The Roaring Twenties

The Roaring Twenties

Sandy Wilson

Eyre Methuen
London

First published 1976
by Eyre Methuen Ltd
11 New Fetter Lane, London EC4P 4EE
Copyright © 1976 Sandy Wilson
Filmset by Keyspools Golborne, Lancs
Printed in Great Britain by
Hazell Watson & Viney Ltd, Aylesbury, Bucks

ISBN 413 32980 1

Picture Credits

Acknowledgements and thanks for permission to reproduce pictures are due to the Radio Times Hulton Picture Library for pages 6, 7, 9–17, 19, 20, 21, 23, 24/25, 27, 28, 33, 34, 35, 56, 58, 70, 71, 78, 79, 84, 90, 95, 101, 102, 103, 110, 111, 112/13, 115, 117, 119–22, 124, 125, 126 and 128 – to the Raymond Mander and John Mitchenson Theatre Collection for pages 22, 31, 41, 64, 66, 67, 68, 69, 72/3, 74, 75, 76, 77, 80/1, 83, 85, 92 and 126 – to the National Film Archive for pages 30, 31, 32, 62, 65, 86, 86/7, 88, 89, 93, 100, 105 and 124 – to Snark International for pages 48, 50, 56, 59, 60, 61 and 95 – to H. Roger-Viollet, Paris, for pages 49, 51–4 and 117 – to the Kodak Museum for pages 78, 114 and 117 – to the Science Museum, London for pages 78/9, 106 and 107 – to Central Press Photos Ltd. for page 68 – to the National Portrait Gallery for page 26 – to Paul Popper for page 36 – to EMI Electronics Ltd. for page 55 – to Ford of Britain for pages 108 and 109 and to the Mary Evans Picture Library for page 110. The picture on the front cover is reproduced by kind permission of the National Film Archive.
No copyright has been wittingly infringed in any picture reproduced in this book.
Grateful thanks are due to Penelope Brown for the picture research.

Introduction

1b

The Roaring Twenties, the Hectic Twenties, the Jazz Decade, the Charleston Era, the Age of the Bright Young Things or the Age of—in Gertrude Stein's resonant phrase—the Lost Generation: whatever name you give them, the Twenties are, of all periods in recent history, the most clearly defined and the most instantly recognisable. Their definition is probably due to the fact that they were bounded at either end by two world catastrophes: the Great War, which ended in November 1918, and the Depression, which began with the Wall Street Crash of October 1929. As a result the decade that came between appears to us today as a kind of lost Paradise, a Garden of Eden whose gates clanged shut for ever at the beginning of the Thirties. On a recent television programme Miss Anita Loos, when asked why the Twenties continued to have such appeal to a generation who could only know of them by hearsay, replied that they were the last time that anybody felt secure. She might have added that they were the last time when anybody felt innocent. For, despite the aura of sophistication that hangs around them, the atmosphere of jazz, cocktails and promis- cuity, the Twenties seem to me an Age of Innocence, a time when Youth could truthfully say, 'Here we are, fresh, eager and unafraid. The future is ours to play with. Let the Games commence!'

These pages are illustrated by three fashion plates: those on the left depict what the well-dressed lady wore to go out to tea in the years before the Great War, that on the right what she wore for the same occasion in the early Thirties. Apart from details of cut and style, there is not much to differentiate between them: wide-brimmed hats, elaborately curled coiffures, long-skirted dresses adorned with frills and flounces—in other words the glorification of 'femininity'. In the following pages you will see how the well-dressed lady—and, indeed, every woman—looked during most of the ten odd years that came between. The change from the pre-Great War period is astounding: one can hardly believe that in a matter of six or seven years the human figure

a

2

could be so transformed. And yet, in as many years later, it was as if this transformation had never taken place. For the truth is that when, in 1929, the Twenties finished with the Crash, they not only came to an end; they were forgotten. It was as if the world had suddenly awoken from a wildly colourful dream, to find itself faced with the bleakness of reality, and the shock quite obliterated the dream for the next twenty years.

I was born in 1924 and, apart from a few vivid sights and, more potently, sounds, I hardly remember the Twenties at all. But I do remember the early Thirties very clearly, and what was remarkable was that, in general, nobody referred to the Twenties or, if they did, it was in a tone of either dismissal, disapproval or ridicule. There seemed to be a sense of guilt about the whole decade, the same sense of guilt as one has had too much to drink the night before but is not quite sure how badly one behaved. Everyone felt a slight unease about the previous ten years: they had had a wonderful party, but it had all been rather too much of a good thing, and now they were paying for it. As a small boy, only dimly aware of what the Depression meant, I found this hard to under-stand, and as the years went by I was drawn irresistibly, as to the garden gate marked 'No Entry', towards what had become almost a Forbidden Decade. Shreds of the old tunes haunted me—how did the Charleston go? A glimpse of a cloche-hatted girl in a photograph beckoned to me, like a Lorelei, from an inaccessible island. Where had it all disappeared to? Why did no-one want to speak about it? While everyone else was busy putting Last Night's Party out of their minds and into the Past, I was making tentative efforts to discover what it had really been like. One day in the local bookshop I came across a copy of Gentlemen Prefer Blondes by Anita Loos, published in 1925. I bought it and read it avidly. My personal rediscovery of the Twenties had begun. . . .

Bye Bye, Blackbird

'Pack up all my care and woe, Here I go, singing low. . . .' One of the British Army's favourite marching songs in 1914 had been 'Pack up your troubles in your old kit-bag', but after four years of a war which, starting out as a crusade against Hun 'frightfulness', turned into a squalid and meaningless ordeal, it must have been hard to raise a smile. When the Armistice finally came, on November 11th 1918, the average man's instinct urged him, despite the politicians' exhortations, to go home, get back to normal and put the spectre of War firmly behind him. BYE BYE, BLACKBIRD, sung by Florence Mills in the Blackbirds Revue, might have been the theme song of the era, but it is significant that its melody was plaintive rather than optimistic. The mood was one of escape—escape from the past, but also, perhaps, from the future—and the carefree rhythm of Jazz, purveyed by black musicians who brought a touch of the exotic into everyone's life, replaced the beat of the marching songs which had led so many thousands to their death.

3. The Western Front, November 12th 1918. On the day after the signing of the Armistice, British soldiers, exhausted by the horrors of trench warfare, greet Peace with a cheer.

4. Victory Day, July 9th 1919.
Processions and street parties
celebrated the signing of the
Peace Treaty; only the left-wing
Daily Herald warned that the
harsh terms meted out to
Germany could lay the
foundations of another war.

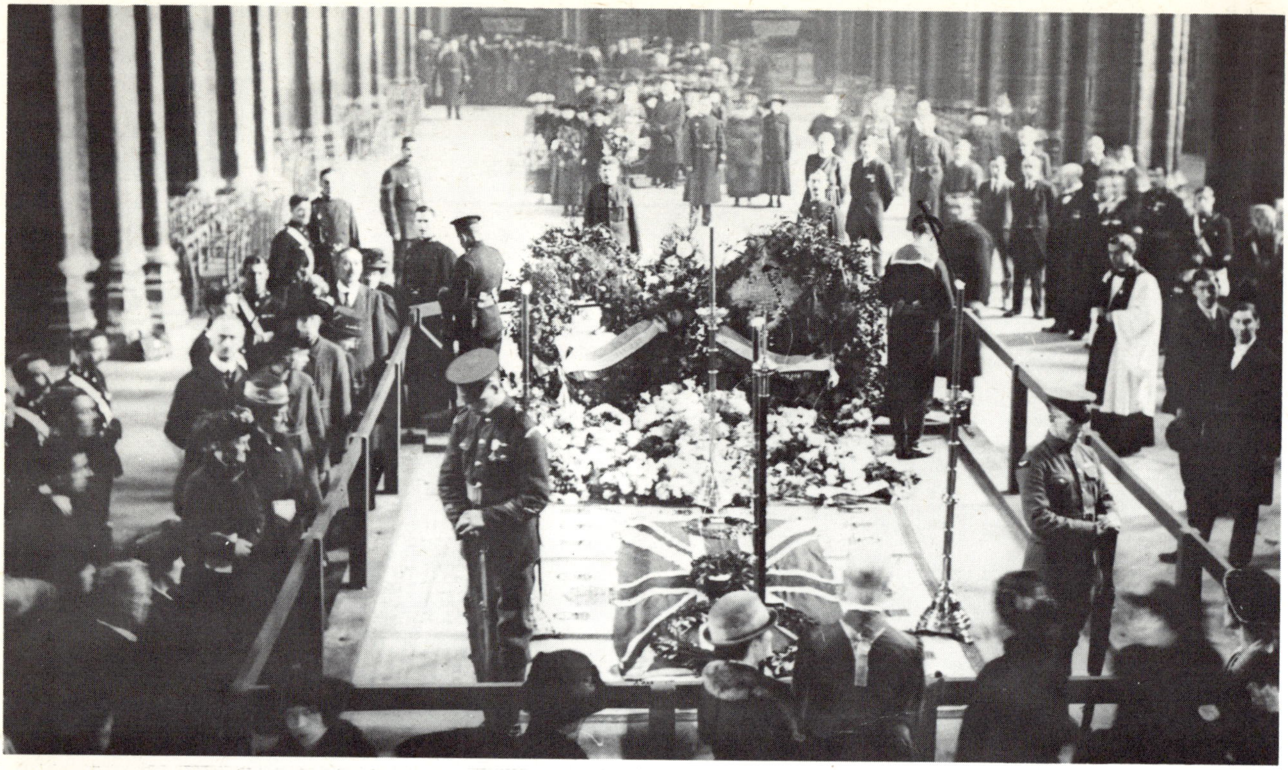

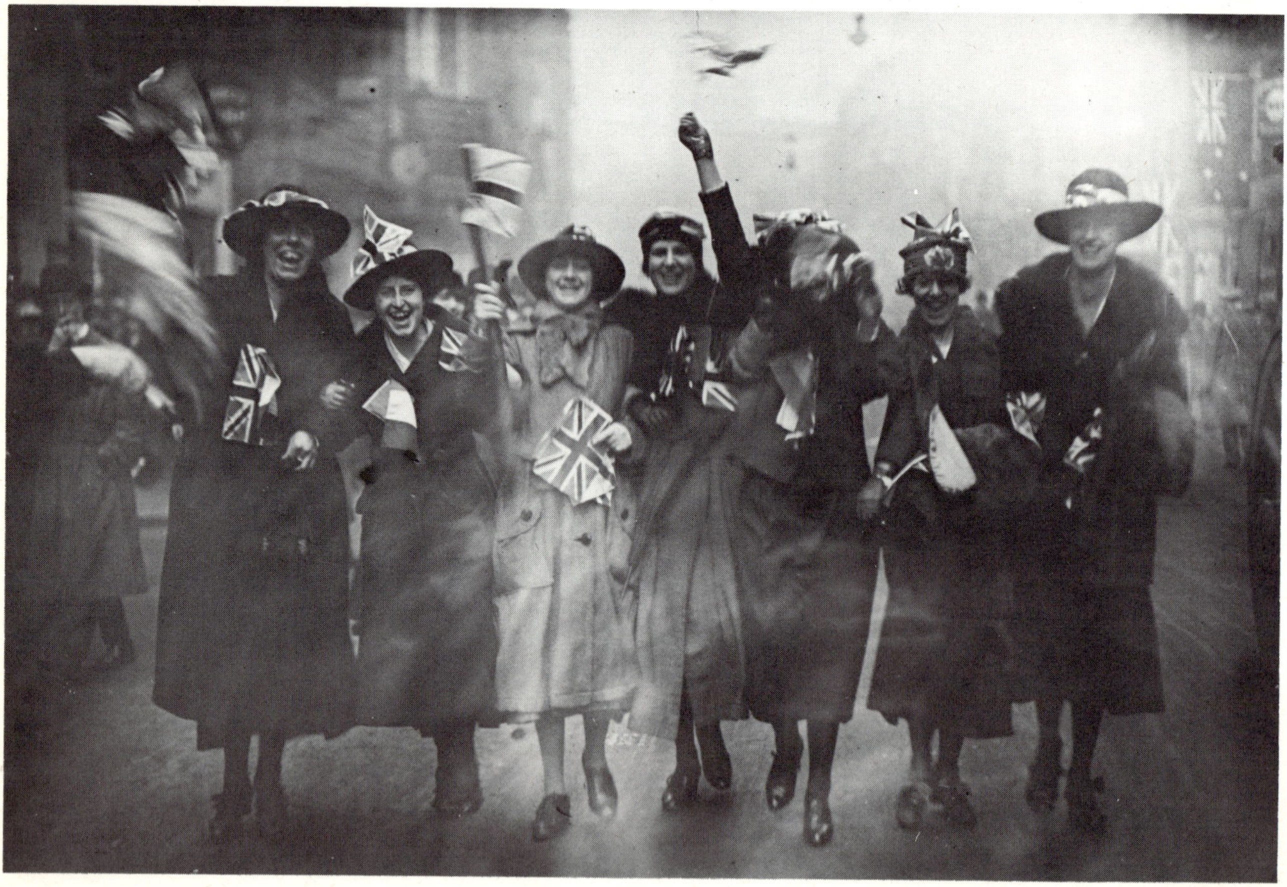

5. On Armistice Day 1920, the body of an Unknown Soldier, brought back from France, was buried in Westminster Abbey, where thousands queued to pay homage.

6. Women workers, to whom the War had brought the beginnings of emancipation, celebrate the coming of Peace.

7. The first session of the Council of the League of Nations at San Sebastian on August 3rd 1920. On the League hung the whole world's hopes for a lasting peace, but by the end of the decade its powers were already eroded.

8. Jazz: emanating from the American South in the early years of the century, during the 1920s it swept through the entire Western world.

9. The Four Harmony Kings: black entertainers and musicians rapidly became the darlings of Society, and no nightclub was complete without a 'nigger band'.

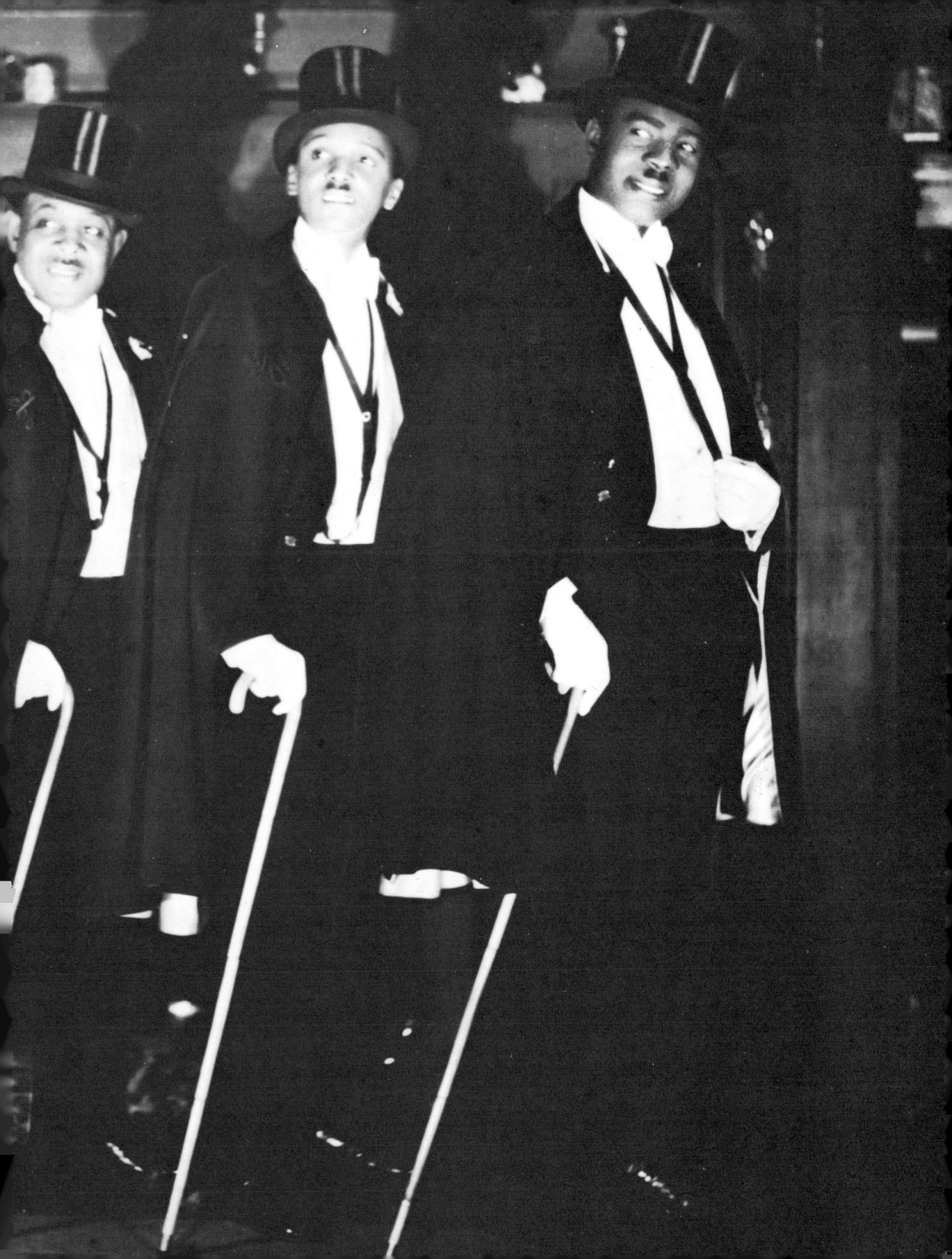

"Ring out the Old—Ring in the New"

An impression by "Fish" of the Café Royal on New Year's Eve

76

10. The Blackbirds Company, photographed on the roof of the London Pavilion in 1926. The stars, Florence Mills, Johnny Hudgins and Edith Wilson, pose with girls of the chorus.

11. New Year's Eve 1920. 'Fish', whose exuberant drawings typified the period, depicts the revels at the Café Royal.

The Girl in the Little Green Hat

'With the wearing of the green
on her head,
I don't care about the life she
has led. . . .'

The original Green Hat belonged,
not to the girl in this Rodgers
and Hart song, but to the
heroine of the novel of the same
name by Michael Arlen, a
naturalised Armenian who made
a fortune from writing trashy, but
stylish, fiction. It was worn 'pour
le sport' and graced the head of
Iris Storm, who did all the things
that other girls longed to but
dared not, such as driving fast
sports cars through Mayfair,
going to bed with a man the
first time she met him, and
whipping off to Paris for the
odd abortion. But, like most
1920s heroines, she was innocent
at heart and paid for her
misdemeanours by crashing into
a tree. 'Above her neck her hair
died a very manly death,' wrote
the narrator, 'a more manly death
than ''bobbed'' hair was ever
known to die'—in other words,
Iris had a 'shingle', which,
together with her long legs, slim
hips and almost imperceptible
bosom, made her the epitome of
all that was desirable in an age
that had turned previous notions
of femininity upside down.

12. Anita Loos, author of
Gentlemen Prefer Blondes,
presents the image of 1920s
womanhood: trim, jaunty and
bubbling with confidence.

13. Even when up to their thighs in the ocean, these bathing beauties do not make the mistake of neglecting their maquillage.

14. At the Royal Academy a gentleman in formal dress looks askance at the girl who applies her lipstick in public—but he was in the minority.

15. Elinor Glyn, author of *Three Weeks*, the novel that shocked pre-War readers, extended her operations to Hollywood in the 1920s—here seen with Ethel Barrymore.

16. A scene from the film of *Three Weeks*: orgies, preferably in fancy dress, were Hollywood's way of deploring vice and at the same time making the most of it.

17. Marie Stopes, the unlikely-looking advocate of contraceptives and birth control. Her book, *Married Love*, was greeted with a storm of abuse and accusations of immorality.

18. Women had been granted the vote in 1918, provided they were over thirty and either married or householders. In 1929 the age was lowered to twenty-one—creating the so-called 'Flapper Vote', to the apparent amusement of the male population.

19. Society women achieved emancipation by going into 'business': Mrs 'Freddie' Cripps opens a hairdressing salon in Bond Street.

20. Mrs Val Gielgud chose the 'masculine' adjuncts of a monocle and an Eton crop . . .

21. . . . . while Suzanne Lenglen, in short skirts and her celebrated bandeau, championed her sex on the tennis court.

22. Despite emancipation, Gloria Swanson (far left), one of Hollywood's most durable stars, never hesitated to employ the standard feminine wiles.

23. On the West End stage, Tallulah Bankhead, madcap daughter of an American senator, was the first actress to have a predominantly female following. 'Gallery girls' shrieked with ecstasy whenever she appeared.

24. Pola Negri (below), statuesque, sultry and exotically gowned, exuded the mysterious quality of continental sex appeal.

25. To describe the attractions of Clara Bow, here impersonating a female 'sheik', Elinor Glyn invented the *mot juste* — 'It'.

26. 'Woman's Pictorial' takes its cue from Hollywood when suggesting designs for its readers to wear to fancy dress parties in 1925.

27. Women may have appropriated men's trousers, but they contrived, in the boudoir at least, to transform them into something incontestably feminine.

28. Two variations on a theme, seen at the races. The bent knee stance, with one hand low on the hip, was basic to 1920s fashion.

29. Pleats, gathers, flares, belts and darts were all brought into play to bring variety to the uniformly tubular silhouette.

30. An adventurous visitor to Longchamps in 1925 appears to have invented her own version of the ubiquitous cloche, while sticking to the current mode in shoes: pointed toes, straps and 'lavatory pedestal' heels.

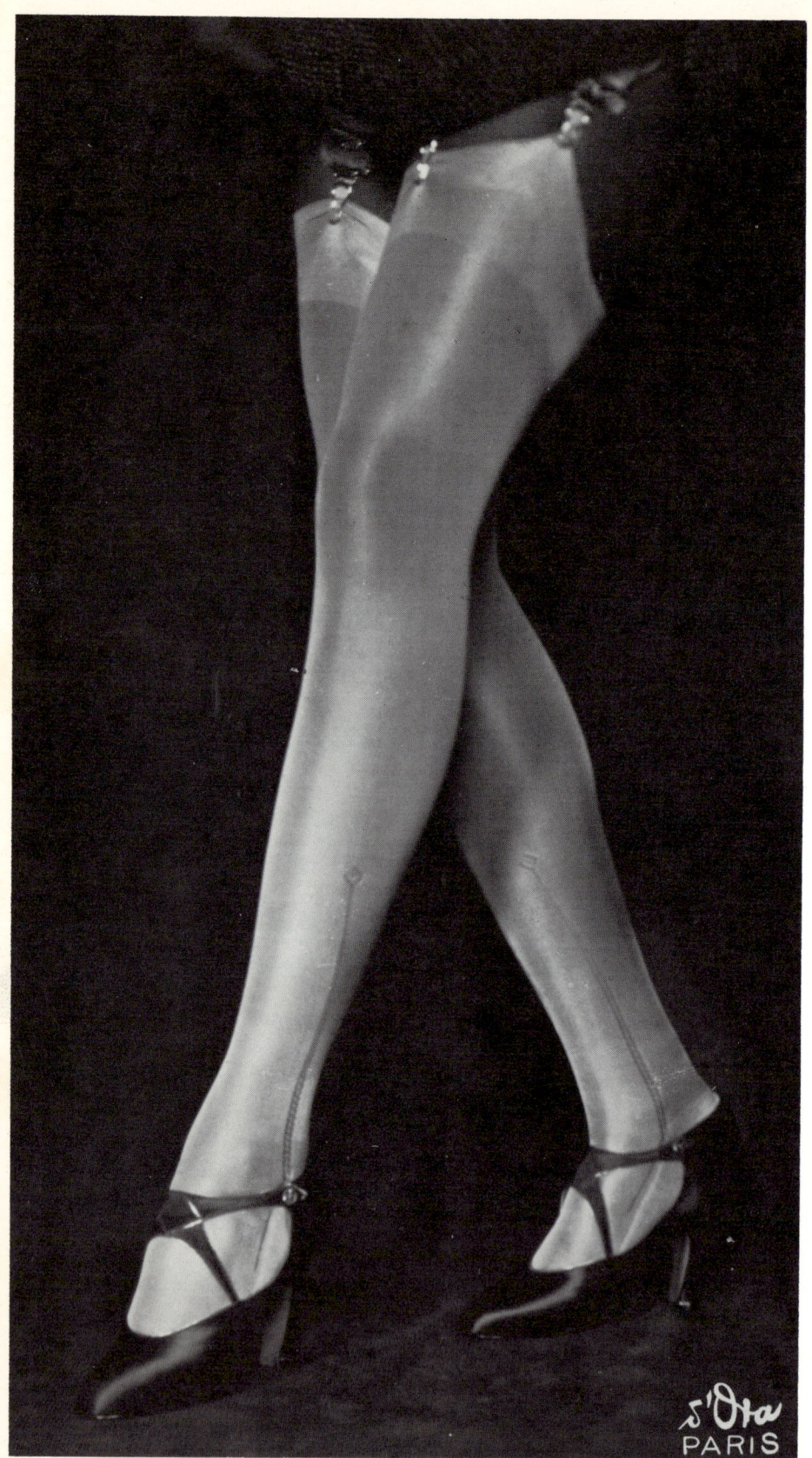

31. The increasing revelation of women's legs brought stockings into focus. These, decorated with 'clocks', adorn the legs of Josephine Baker; for the rest of her, see 53.

32. Feminine lingerie, once a mass of flounces, whale-bone and padding, had to be brought into line with the slim silhouette, but decoration still ran riot.

d'Ora
PARIS

LOVELY FABRICS MAKE THE NEW LINGERIE.

Her silhouette must be straight, and so must her undies, hence Peter Robinson, Oxford Street, has created this pale pink crêpe-de-chine Princess petticoat with a net corsage, with motifs of crêpe-de-chine. The cap is en suite

There is something particularly fascinating about this triple ninon set, sketched at Coulson's, 105, New Bond Street, W., its charm enhanced with drawn-thread work and satin bows

Snow-white nainsook shows just how fascinating it can be in alliance with lace in this cami-knicker that is sojourning at P. Steinmann and Co.'s, 185, Piccadilly, W.

This pretty Bel-Broid nightie is of tarantulle; it is hand embroidered and threaded with satin ribbon. The Belgembroid Lingerie Co., Monaghan, will send particulars of their Bel-Broid lingerie. It is charming

Olive Herverdine

33. As winter sports became
fashionable, designers began to
create appropriate clothes for
both participants and spectators.

34. A new garment for a new
activity : the cocktail dress was
now an indispensable item in the
fashionable woman's wardrobe —
this one is accompanied by a
matching vanity bag, worn on the
wrist.

35. An electric hair-dryer enabled a young lady to have a shampoo at home; even so, its manipulation was left to the lady's maid.

36. Cochran's Young Ladies, featured in his new revue, demonstrate every variety of hairstyle, from the 'bob' to the 'perm' to the 'shingle'.

Off with the Hair and "On with the Dance!"

THE LONG AND THE SHORT OF IT: MISS BERONIUS, WITH A CHIGNON; MISS DESMOND, IN VICTORIAN MOOD: AND MISS VARDA, WITH HER ETON SHINGLE.

WAVES, A CURLY MOP, AND A FRINGED, STRAIGHT SHINGLE: MISS NURICK, MISS MOWBRAY, AND MISS BARBOWA.

37. Charles Lindbergh, when he flew the Atlantic, became an international idol and the cloche hat began to imitate the aviator's helmet.

38. By 1928 every vestige of hair had disappeared beneath the cloche's brim — and in profile the eyes sometimes vanished as well.

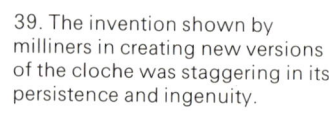

39. The invention shown by milliners in creating new versions of the cloche was staggering in its persistence and ingenuity.

40. Anita Loos' heroine, Lorelei Lee, saw past the fleeting foibles of fashion and took a firm grip on essentials.

"Kissing your hand may make you feel very good but a diamond bracelet lasts forever."

Parisian Pierrot

'. . . . Society's hero,
The Rue de la Paix
Is under your sway. . . .'

Or, to put it another way, 'How're we gonna keep them down on the farm, Now that they've seen Paree?' In the Edwardian era Henry James immortalised the American innocent abroad, but his visitors to Europe were usually of good family and invariably well-heeled. The USA's entry into the War in 1917 enabled thousands of 'doughboys' to travel Over There, who otherwise would probably never have left their home towns, and many of them, once they had acquired a taste for European culture, lost no time in returning as soon as the War was over. What was more, the living was cheap, there was no Prohibition, and a fellow could live it up in a way that would never have been tolerated west of Chicago. The most celebrated of these aesthetic emigrés, and more Harlequin than Pierrot, was F. Scott Fitzgerald, whose Columbine was the tragic Zelda. Europe was their downfall, but for the young Ernest Hemingway 'Paris was always worth it' — a dictum which may not hold good today but which, for the 1920s, was an indisputable truth.

41. Gertrude Lawrence sang Noël Coward's number for the first time in André Charlot's revue, LONDON CALLING, at the Duke of York's Theatre in 1923.

GERTRUDE
LAWRENCE
AS PIERROT

" The world may flatter,
But what does that matter,
They'll never shatter
Your gloom profound
Parisian Pierrot.
Your spirits at zero
Divinely forlorn.
With exquisite scorn
From sunset to dawn."

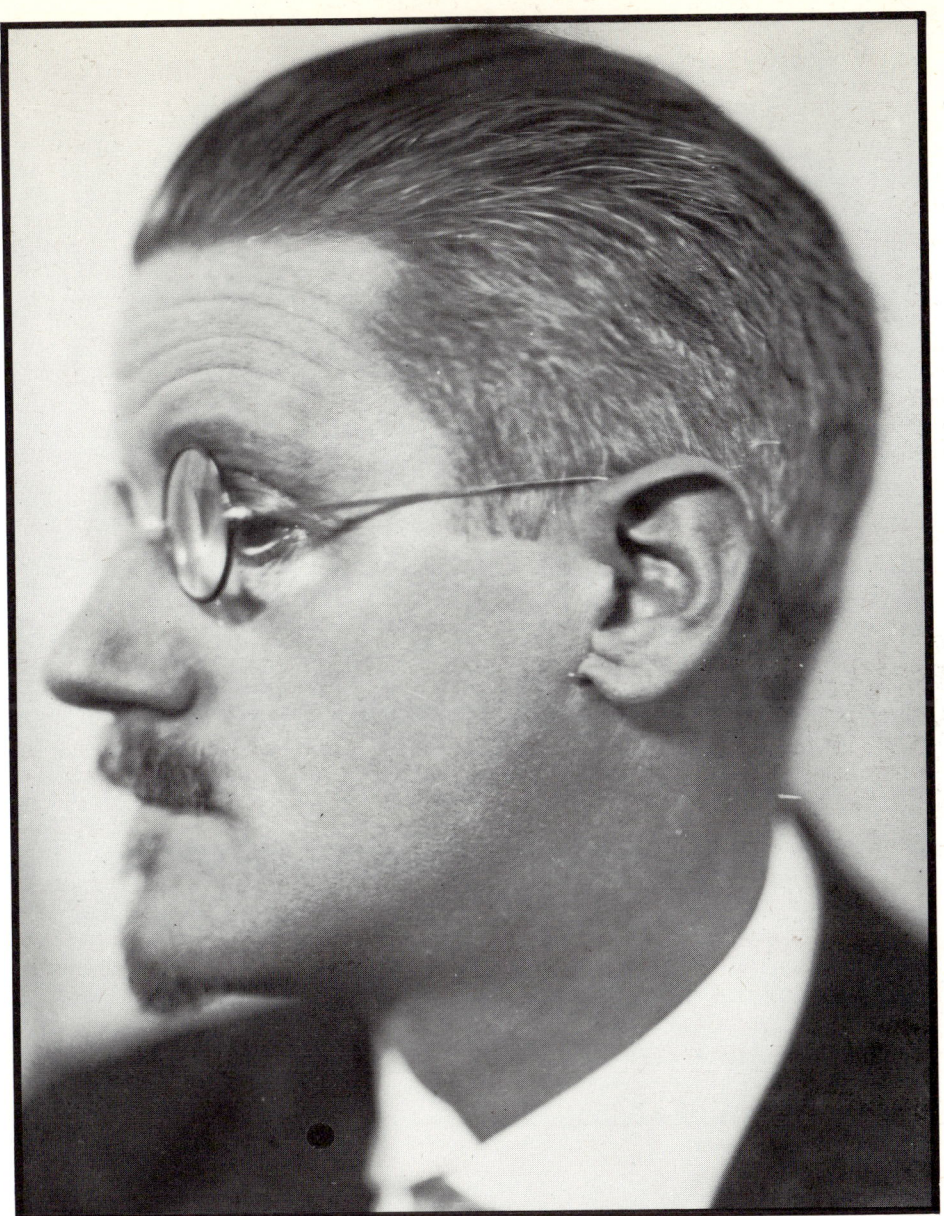

42. The novelist, F. Scott
Fitzgerald, at the height of his
fame, celebrating Christmas 1925
with his wife, Zelda, and their
daughter, Scottie, in their Paris
apartment.

43. When his novel, *Ulysses*, was
published in Paris in 1922, James
Joyce achieved notoriety both for
its revolutionary style and its
liberal use of hitherto forbidden
words.

44. Picasso's powerful portrait of
Gertrude Stein, to whose salon in
the Rue de Fleurus flocked most
of the celebrated writers and
artists of the period.

45. Visitors to the cafés of Paris's
Latin Quarter still believed they
might pick up an undiscovered
masterpiece for a few francs.

46. Le Select in the mid-
Twenties: one of several side-
walk cafés where American
emigrés met to exchange news,
read each other's writings or just
gossip.

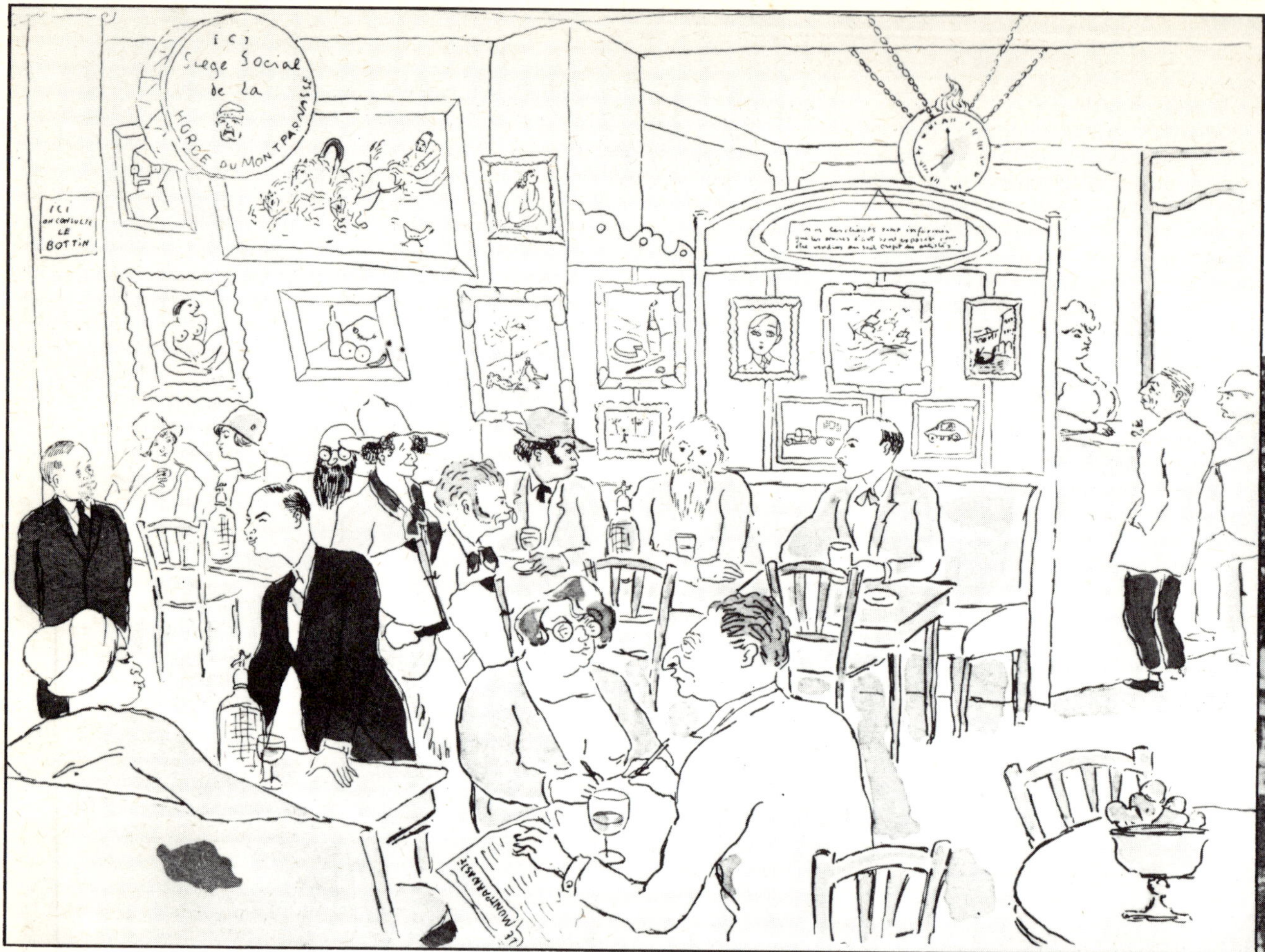
Ici
Siège Social
de la
Horde du Montparnasse
Ici
on consulte
le
Bottin
Le Montparnasse

SHAKESPEARE AND COMPANY
SHAKESPEARE AND COMPANY
LENDING LIBRARY
BOOKSHOP

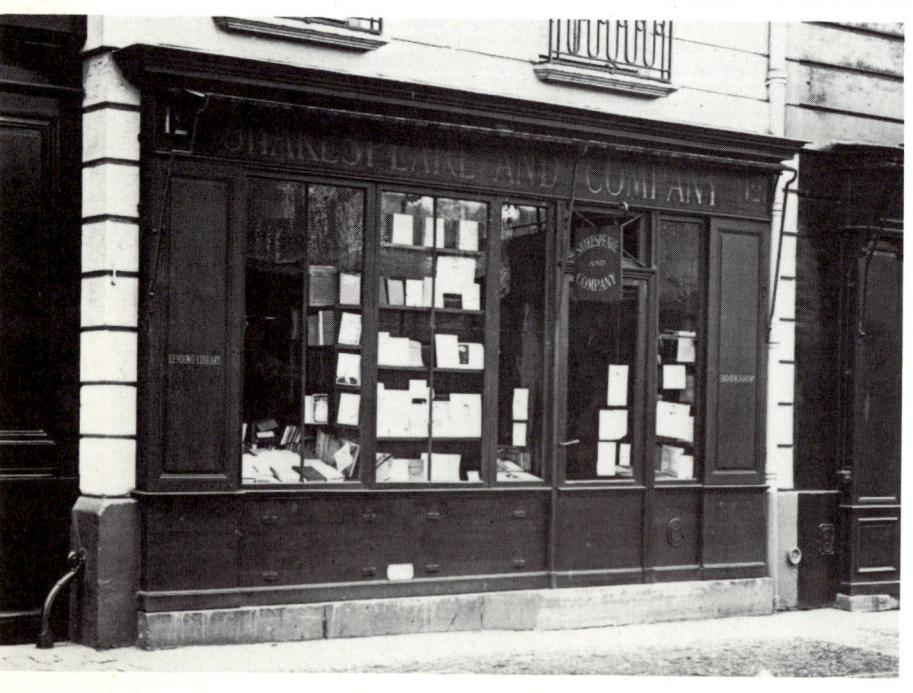

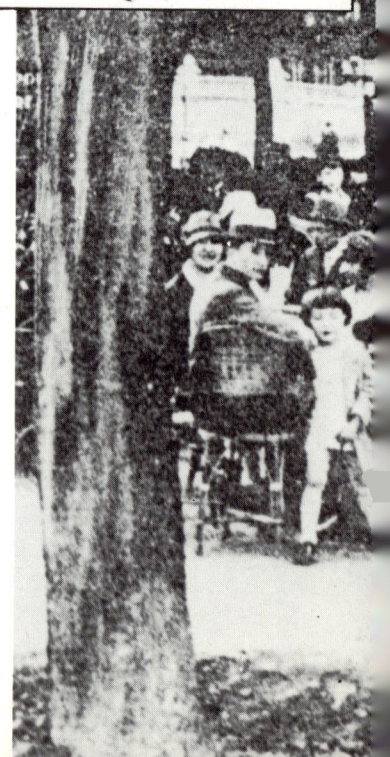

47. Local artists caricatured in a Montparnasse café: the notice reads, 'Customers are informed that the works of art are for sale for the sole profit of the painters.'

48. The English book-shop, Shakespeare & Company, in the Rue de Tournon, whose proprietress, Sylvia Beach, allowed the impoverished Hemingway to run up an account.

49. La Closerie de Lilas: Hemingway, who often went there to write, described it as 'warm inside in the winter and spring and fine outside in the fall.'

50. The Scott Fitzgeralds, with their friends, the Gerald Murphys, pioneered the popularisation of the French Riviera as a summer resort.

51. The Terrace at Monte Carlo in 1924: previous to the American invasion, it was favoured by the English for winter holidays.

52. A Parisian cabaret in 1925: unrestricted drinking and uninhibited entertainment were the attractions for American visitors.

53. Josephine Baker, a New York negress who conquered Paris in the Folies Bergère, wearing her sensational 'banana' costume.

54. Maurice Chevalier became in the Twenties, and later on screen in the Thirties, the epitome of what the Americans felt a Frenchman ought to be.

CASINO DE PARIS

55. Mistinguett, drawn for a poster by Cappiello: her talent was small, but her personality formidable, and her legs were insured for thousands of francs.

56. Erté's designs for spectacular Parisian revues managed to combine elegance, extravagance and sensuality to a degree never since equalled.

57. Thanks to the portable gramophone, everybody's dancing daughters could imagine themselves to be Joan Crawford wherever and whenever they pleased.

58. Customers queue to have their gramophone records signed by the musicians who made them.

Dance, Little Lady

'Time is fleeting
To the rhythm beating in your
mind. . .'

When, in OUR DANCING DAUGHTERS, Joan Crawford as 'Dangerous Diana' tossed off her frock and Charlestoned in her undies to keep the party going, she was symbolising a generation for whom dancing was not so much a passion as an obsession. The craze had begun well before 1914, when hotels and restaurants first installed orchestras for their customers to dance to, and was fostered in the hectic atmosphere of war-time; but it was in the Twenties that it reached its zenith and in the Charleston itself that it achieved an apotheosis. This dance had as its essence a thrusting second beat to the bar which impelled its performers to kick out one leg at right angles while the opposite ankle twisted in reverse — a knack which was so essential to acquire that people could be seen practising in bus queues and on station platforms. At first it was condemned as decadent, but even the older generation sanctioned it on hearing that the Prince of Wales turned up at the Café de Paris at 10 a.m. for his Charleston lessons.

59. The Palais de Danse, a temple dedicated to the new craze, opened its doors in every big city in the country.

60. Rudolph Valentino rehearses the Tango — the dance which was to launch him to instant fame in the film of Ibanez' THE FOUR HORSEMEN OF THE APOCALYPSE.

61. Valentino-style tango-dancers proliferated: here Addison Fowler partners Florenz Tamara in cabaret at the Kit Kat Club.

62. Most of Hollywood's stars were called upon to dance: Nancy Carroll (top l.) demonstrates the Varsity Drag, and even Myrna Loy (r.), later to be famous for polished comedy, had to kick up her heels.

RISING STARS: YOUTH AND BEAUTY ON THE SCREEN.

"THE VARSITY DRAG": NANCY CARROLL, OF PARAMOUNT, DEMONSTRATES THE LATEST DANCE.

WE DANCING MODERNS: MYRNA LOY, THE WARNER STAR, PERSONIFIES THE JAZZ AGE.

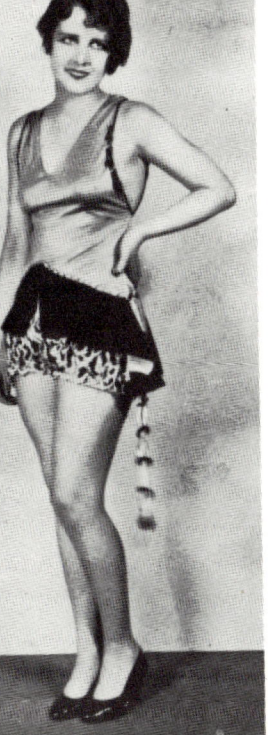

COSTUMED FOR THE BEACH: ANITA PAGE, THE YOUNG ACTRESS OF METRO-GOLDWYN MAYER FILMS.

A SCREEN RECRUIT FROM THE "LEGITIMATE": MARY DUNCAN, WHO PLAYED IN THE PRODUCTION OF "THE SHANGHAI GESTURE" IN NEW YORK FOR THREE YEARS.

FORMERLY OF THE ZIEGFELD FOLLIES AGNES FRANEY, NOW PLAYING IN WARNER PICTURES.

All members of the younger guard, these clever and beautiful young people are all, at the moment, knocking insistently at the door of first-class film fame. Miss Agnes Franey, the youngest of them all, is only eighteen and was signed on by the Warner Company while she was playing in the Ziegfeld production, "Rio Rita." Miss Mary Duncan, who has now signed a screen contract with the Fox Company, is a well-known New York actress and has played for three years in that city in "The Shanghai Gesture."

ROYAL ALBERT HALL

CHARLES B. COCHRAN GENERAL MANAGER

CHARLESTON BALL AND COMPETITION

WEDNESDAY · DECEMBER · 15 · 1926

LONDON PAVILION

CHARLES B. COCHRAN

presents

FLORENCE MILLS

in

LEW LESLIE'S

"BLACKBIRDS"

including

JOHNNY HUDGINS'

PLANTATION BAND

SHRIMP JONES
Leader

JOHNNY DUNN
Creator of the "Wa Wa"

PIKE DAVIS
First Cornet

63. When the Charleston arrived in England in 1925, it was received by sixty dancing instructors at the Carnival Club in Dean Street. Here it is demonstrated by the man who introduced it, Santos Casani.

64. Charleston contests, such as this one at the Albert Hall, helped to popularise the dance throughout the country.

65. Noël Coward and Gertrude
Lawrence, in LONDON
CALLING, give an imitation
of. . . .

66. . . . . Fred and Adele Astaire,
the brother and sister dance team
who enchanted London when
they did the Oom-Pa Trot in
STOP FLIRTING at the
Shaftesbury Theatre in 1923.

67. In the second edition of THE
BLACKBIRDS Edith Wilson
demonstrated a new dance, the
Black Bottom: the title referred to
the Mississippi river-bed and not
to the dancer's posterior.

68. But the upper classes
preferred more sedate dances
such as the slow fox-trot, when
they attended an all-night ball on
the 'World's biggest liner', the
MAJESTIC.

69. No musical comedy was complete without a line of high-kicking chorus girls, who were sent on whenever the plot threatened to collapse: these are from Jack Buchanan's THAT'S A GOOD GIRL.

70. Rosy and Jenny, the Dolly Sisters from Hungary, were two of the most bizarre entertainers of the period: here they are being driven in tandem by Clifton Webb, in Cochran's 1921 revue, THE FUN OF THE FAYRE.

71. Musical comedy romance depended on the unlikeliest of encounters. The gentleman at the wheel is George Clarke.

72. 'You Can Dance with Any Girl At All'. Irene Browne and George Grossmith perform one of the hits from NO, NO, NANETTE at the Palace Theatre, 1925.

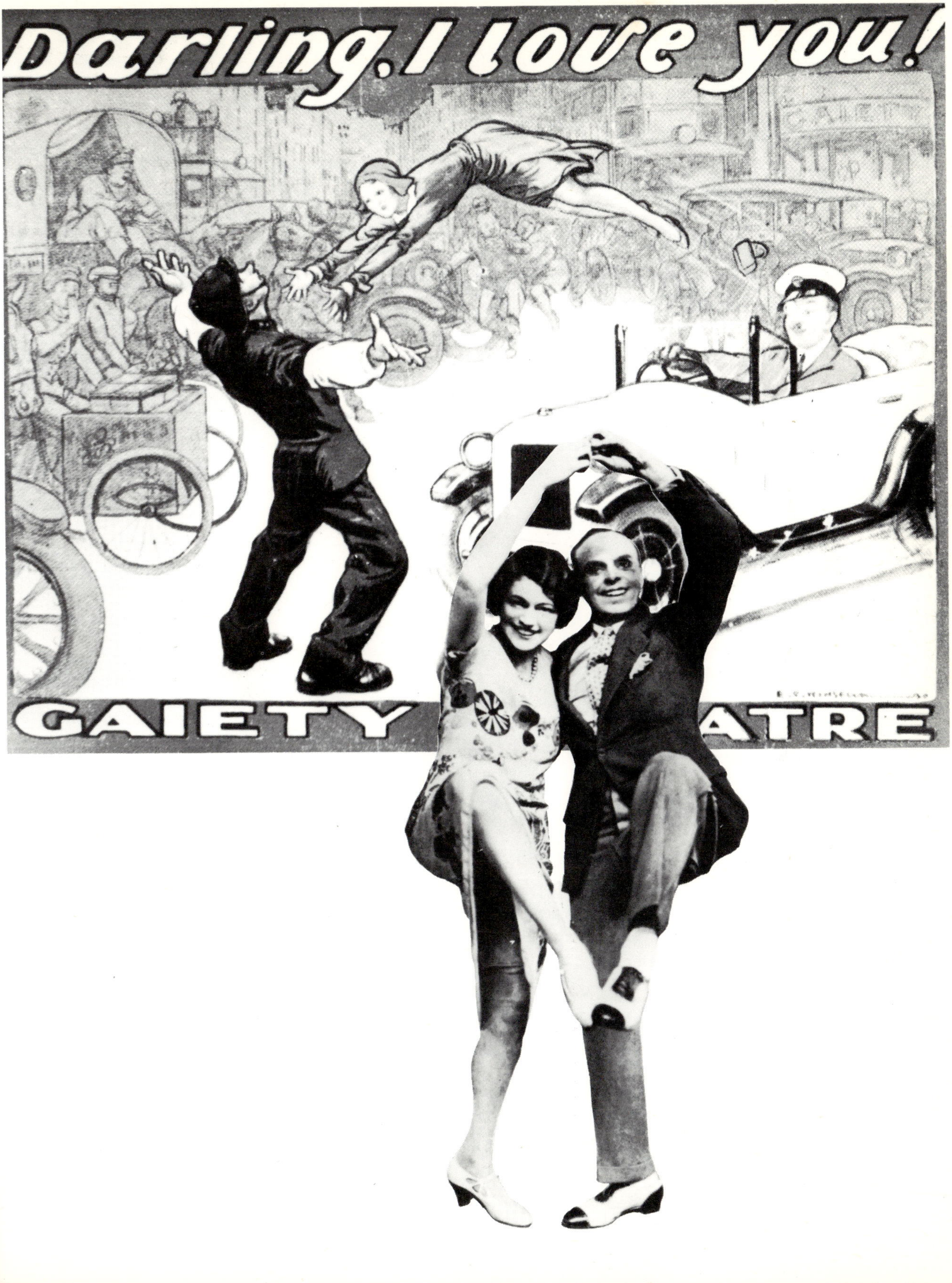
Darling. I love you!
GAIETY
ATRE

73. MERCENARY MARY starred Peggy O'Neil and had songs with titles like 'Tie A String Around Your Finger, Dear'; 'Charleston Mad', and 'Honey, I'm In Love With You'.

74. Jessie Matthews and Sonnie Hale dance to Noël Coward's 'Try To Learn To Love' in Cochran's revue, THIS YEAR OF GRACE, at the London Pavilion, 1928.

75. A new craze, the wireless set,
brought the sounds of the world
into everyone's home.

76 The Last Post is played (left)
on Armistice Day 1923 from
London's radio station, 2LO, the
fore-runner of Broadcasting
House.

77. Early wireless sets required
earphones, which were shared
out amongst the family — whether
they liked it or not.

78 The couple below are
listening in to a concert from the
Eiffel Tower while driving round
Paris in a taxi cab.

Wife: What shall I put on now, sweetie?
Husband (who has had his fill): *The Lid!* for the love of Mike!

79. In the search for novelty,
dance bands assumed every kind
of guise: this one is Gwen Rogers
and her Romany Players. . . .

80. . . . . whose recordings of the
latest hits could well have caused
the husband's outburst in
Sherwood's Tatler cartoon.

The Sheik of Araby

'O Sheik of Ara-bee
(Yes a bee, yes a bee, not a wasp)'

The 1920s' infatuation with the Sheik — the nomad chieftain whose one aim in life, it was firmly believed, was to carry young ladies off into the desert and wreak his will upon them under canvas — had its origin in a novel of that name by an otherwise forgotten writer, E. M. Hull. The word passed into the language as a synonym for 'boy-friend', and Hollywood did its best to supply screen personifications of this dream lover, who had to be dark (blond hair did not, in any case, photograph well), flashing-eyed and, as the fan magazines frankly insisted, beautiful. The most beautiful of them all was an Italian dancing-partner turned actor, Rudolph Valentino: he also had a magnificent body, moved like a panther, and could, with one side-long glance, convey more sex than all the explicit grunting and heaving of today. When he died in 1926, his funeral stopped the traffic, and for years afterwards a mysterious veiled lady placed roses on his grave.

81. In Sigmund Romberg's operetta the heroine was abducted by a sheik called the Red Shadow. But in reality he was an officer in the Foreign Legion, so all ended happily.

THE DESERT SONG

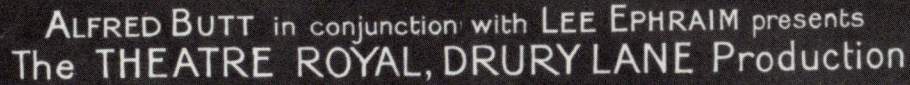

ALFRED BUTT in conjunction with LEE EPHRAIM presents
The THEATRE ROYAL, DRURY LANE Production

The DESERT SONG

BOOK & LYRICS BY
OTTO HARBACH
OSCAR HAMMERSTEIN 2ND
& FRANK MANDEL
MUSIC BY
SIGMUND ROMBERG

SEPARATE NUMBERS

	PRICE
The Desert Song	2/- NET
Romance	2/- "
The Riff Song	2/- "
"It"	2/- "
One Alone	2/- "
One Flower grows alone in Your Garden	2/- "
Piano Selection	2/6 NET
Desert Song Valse	2/- "

CHAPPELL & CO LTD
50 NEW BOND STREET, LONDON, W.I.
& SYDNEY

HARMS INCORPORATED
62 & 64 WEST 45TH STREET
NEW YORK

82. Rudolph Valentino and Vilma Banky in THE SON OF THE SHEIK. Valentino's sex appeal was usually spiced with a discreet suggestion of sadism.

83. When he was not baring his chest, 'Rudi' often went to the other extreme, as on the left, in THE YOUNG RAJAH.

84. . . . . or below, in MONSIEUR BEAUCAIRE, whose sets and costumes set new standards of picturesque lavishness.

85. But, just to prove that he was a normal man at heart, the studio released this still of Valentino relaxing with a good book.

86. The entrance that heralded the birth of a star: Valentino in THE FOUR HORSEMEN OF THE APOCALYPSE, made in 1921

87. Another Latin Lover: Ricardo Cortez played opposite Greta Garbo in ANNA KARENINA, but was sacked halfway through the shooting and replaced by John Gilbert.

88. The teaming of Garbo and Gilbert was given added piquancy by reports of their real-life romance.

89. Douglas Fairbanks Senior takes time off from filming THE BLACK PIRATE to pose for a statuette. His physical grace more than made up for his deficiencies as an actor.

90. The Apache was the Paris Underworld's equivalent of the Sheik. Carl Brisson portrays him, dancing with his sister, Tilly, while Dorothy Ward faints in the arms of her husband, Shaun Glenville.

"THE APACHE"—AND FRIENDS!

№ 1482.
6d EDITION
ISSUED IN CONJUNCTION WITH THE "FELIX THE CAT" CARTOONS
APPEARING EXCLUSIVELY IN Pathès "EVE & EVERYBODY'S
FILM REVIEW.
FELIX
KEPT
ON
WALKING
WORDS BY
Ed. E. BRYANT
MUSIC BY
HUBERT W. DAVID
Copyright.
Price 6d net
Lawrence Wright

SUBSCRIBER'S COPY.
ISSUED IN CONJUNCTION WITH THE NEW GAUMONT MIRROR
CARTOON.
№ 1698
DISMAL DESMOND
FOX-TROT SONG
Written & Composed
BY
RICHARD ELLETT
BILLIE GREY
EDDIE STAMPER
AND
EVERETT LYNTON
PRICE 6D NET
Lawrence Wright.

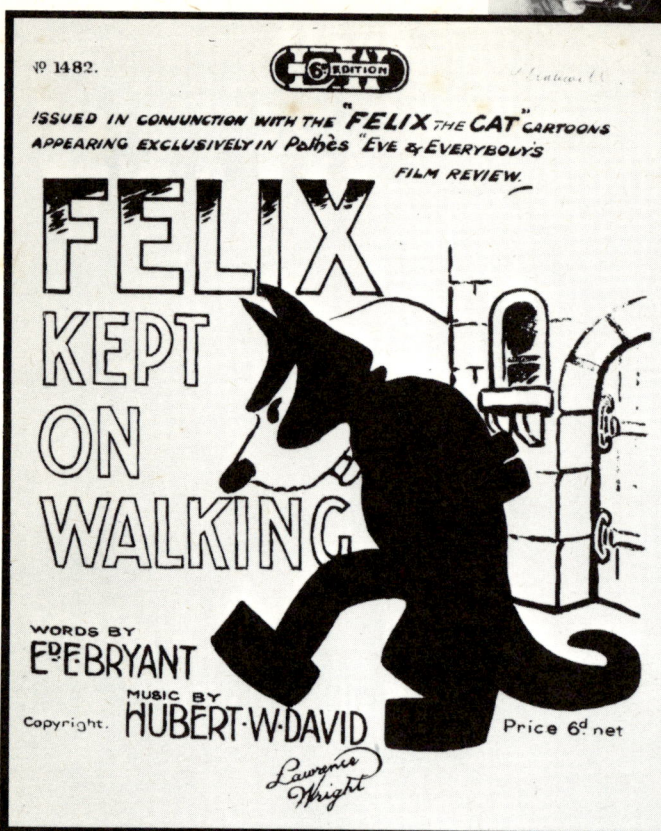

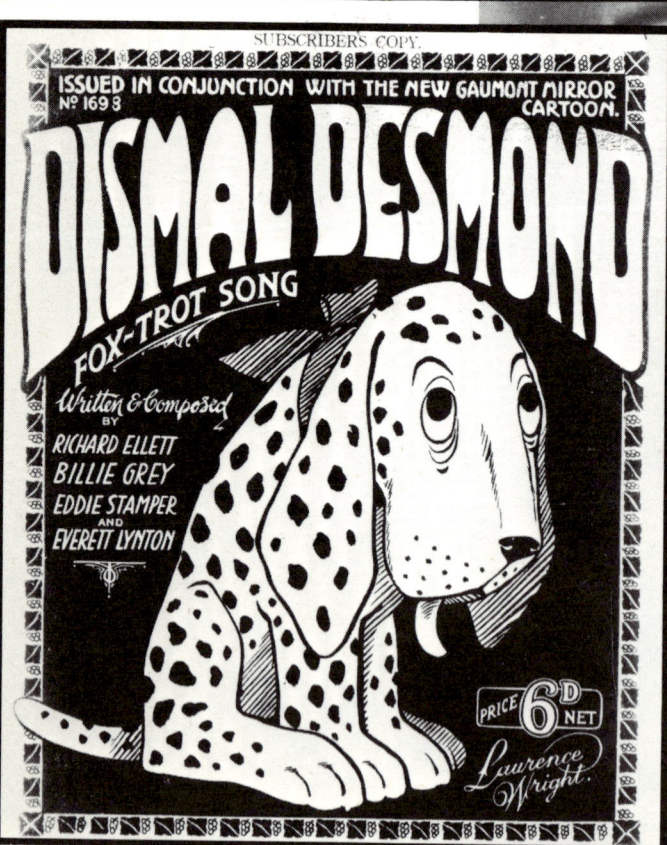

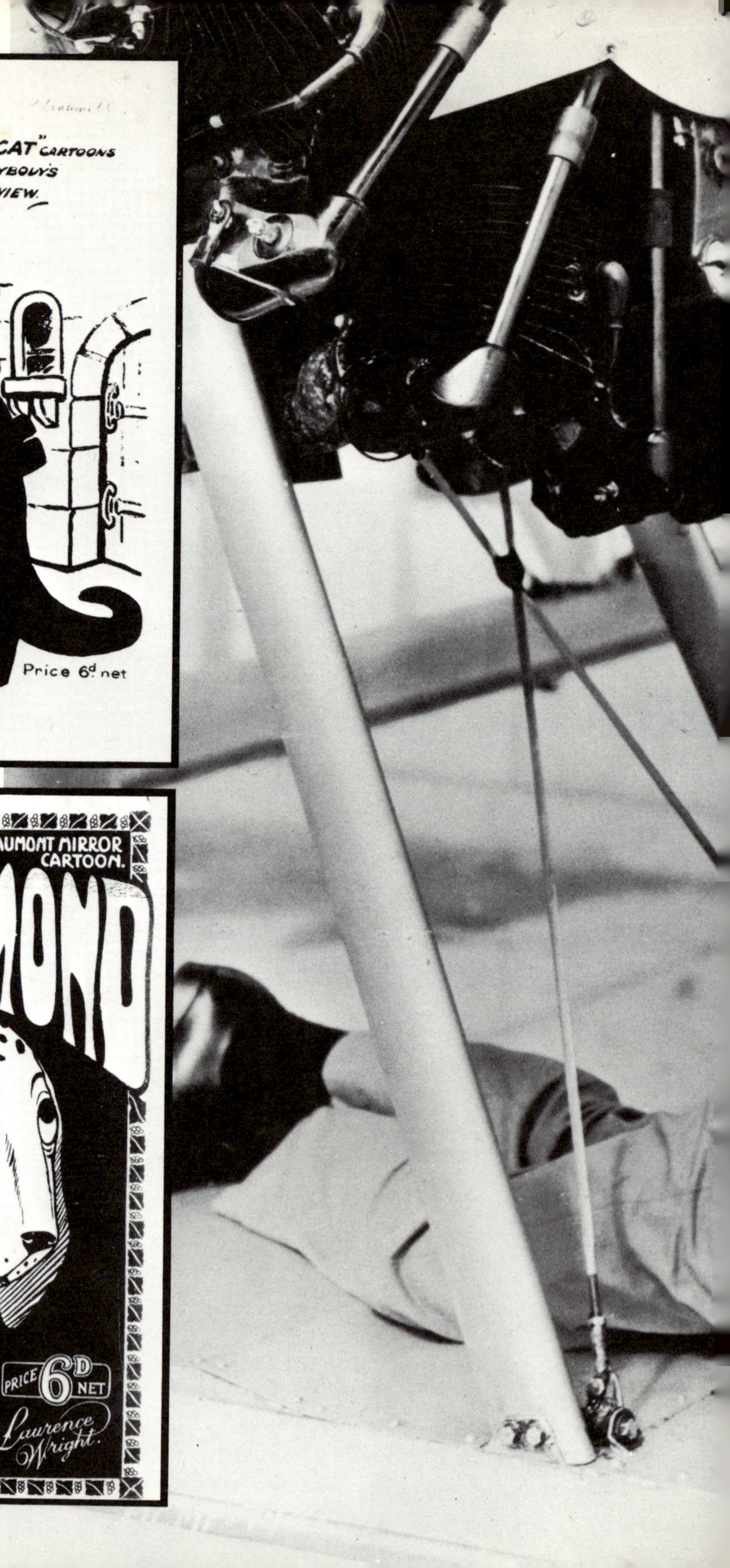

91. Animal heroes on the screen had as loyal a following as human ones. Felix the Cat's cartoons lasted into the early days of the Talkies.

92. Dismal Desmond was Felix's British rival and also had a song dedicated to him.

93. Ramon Novarro, groomed as a successor to Valentino, made his name in MGM's super-colossal 1926 film version of BEN HUR.

94. Twenties Heroes in other walks of life. Charles Lindbergh's plane, the Spirit of St Louis, in which he flew the Atlantic solo in May 1927.

95. 'Lindy', with his boyish good looks and diffident manner, became as great a public idol as any film star.

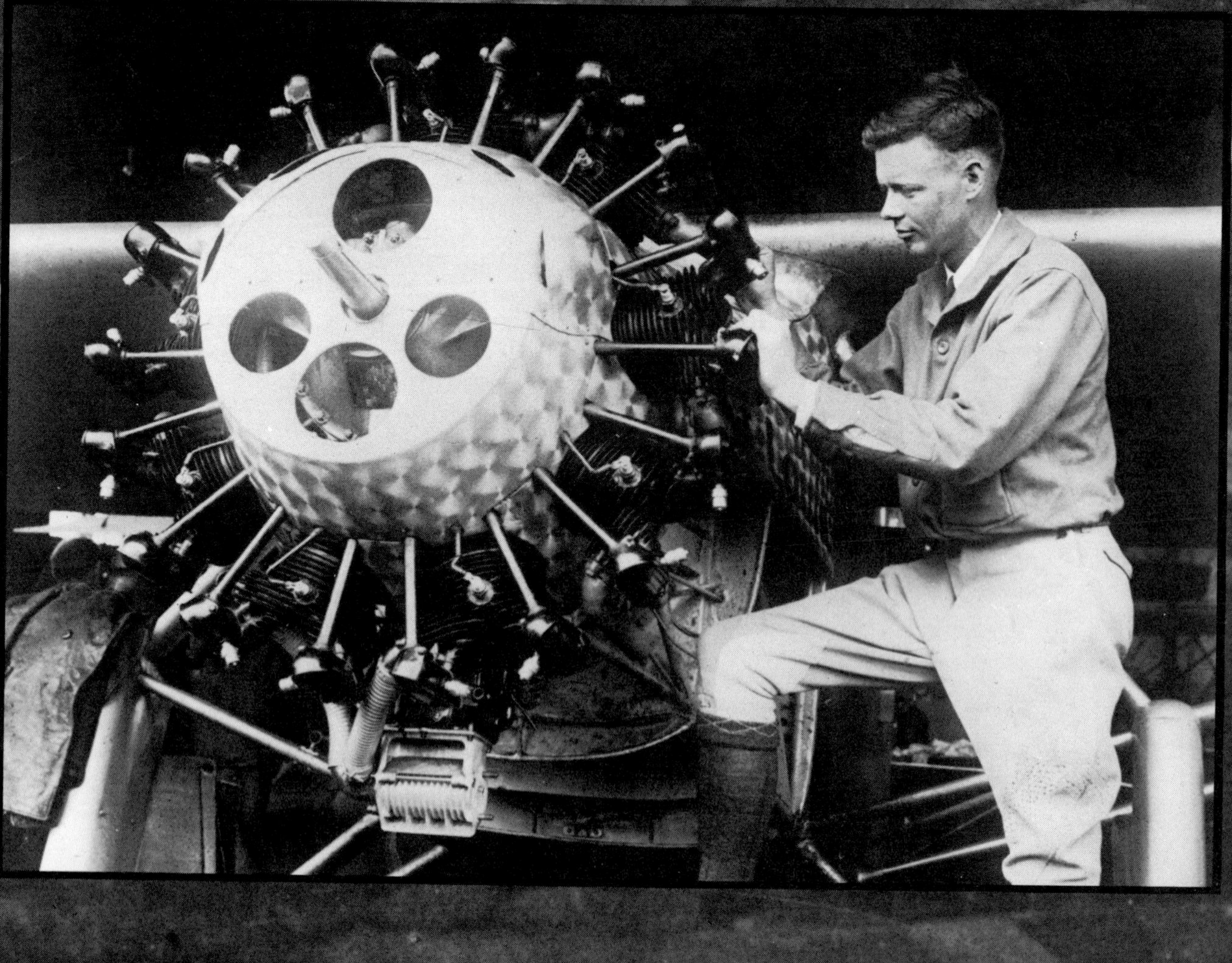

96. Babe Ruth, American base-
ball player, achieved the
distinction of having a candy bar
named after him.

97. Georges Carpentier was not
only a champion boxer; he was
so beautiful that women would
faint at the ringside.

98. Golf, hitherto an upper-class
sport, began to find popularity
with the masses during the
1920s. Bobby Jones puts in some
practice for St Andrews.

À L'ÉCRAN
LE GRAND MATCH SENSATIONNEL
CARPENTIER-COOK
POUR LE CHAMPIONNAT D'EUROPE
Gaumont CONCESSIONNAIRE

99. The 1920s' most popular hero: the Prince of Wales.

100. Throughout the decade the Prince toured the world as a travelling salesman for the Monarchy. This off-duty snap with Lord Louis Mountbatten was taken in New Zealand.

101. Dressing up was part of the job: the Prince dons the regalia of a Maori chieftain. . . .

102. . . . . and, in Canada, he makes a slightly wistful Red Indian Brave.

The *Duty* of Flirtation

"FLIRTATION," says Uncle Boo, *" is like an exquisite wine whose perfection only the most sensitive palate can detect. As practised by the gallants of the eighteen-eighties it was the most delicate kind of conversational skating over thin ice. But to-day we have no thin ice: we have nothing between an iron frost and a rapid thaw. In short, we have no manners, by gad ! "*

By
Gerald Bullett

" Some public-spirited person will organise Flirtation Classes all over the country "

103. 'Lounge Lizard' was the nice name for a gigolo. Joan Crawford accepts cocktails from three of the species, but managed to retain her virginity unti the last reel.

104. A magazine article suggests that the modern lover could benefit from a course in the Victorian art of Flirtation.

105. 'What the Well-Dressed Man is Wearing'. These male models at a fashion show in Nottingham (top right) totally lack the self-assurance of their present-day counterparts.

106. 'Plus-fours' were a longer version of the Victorian knickerbocker. Originally worn for golf, they quickly became fashionable in other settings, and, in the next decade, as quickly disappeared.

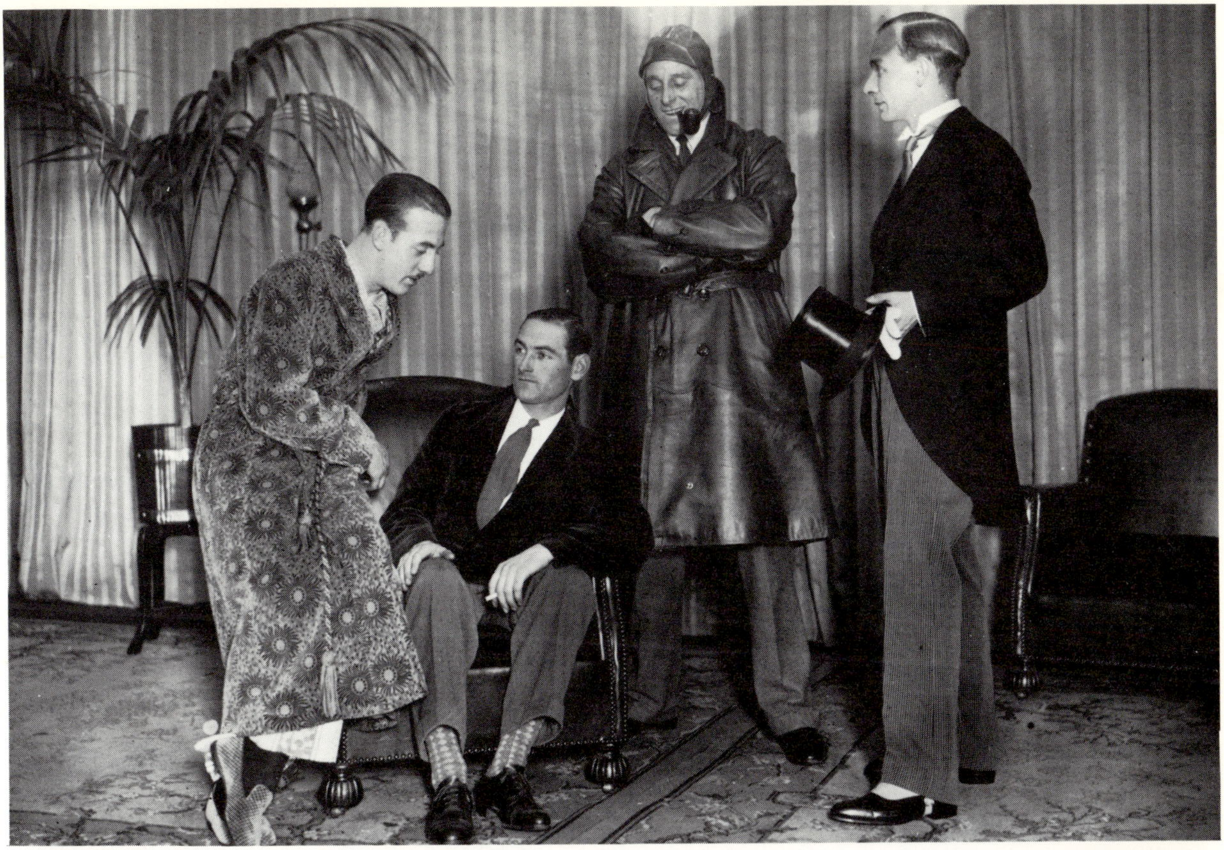

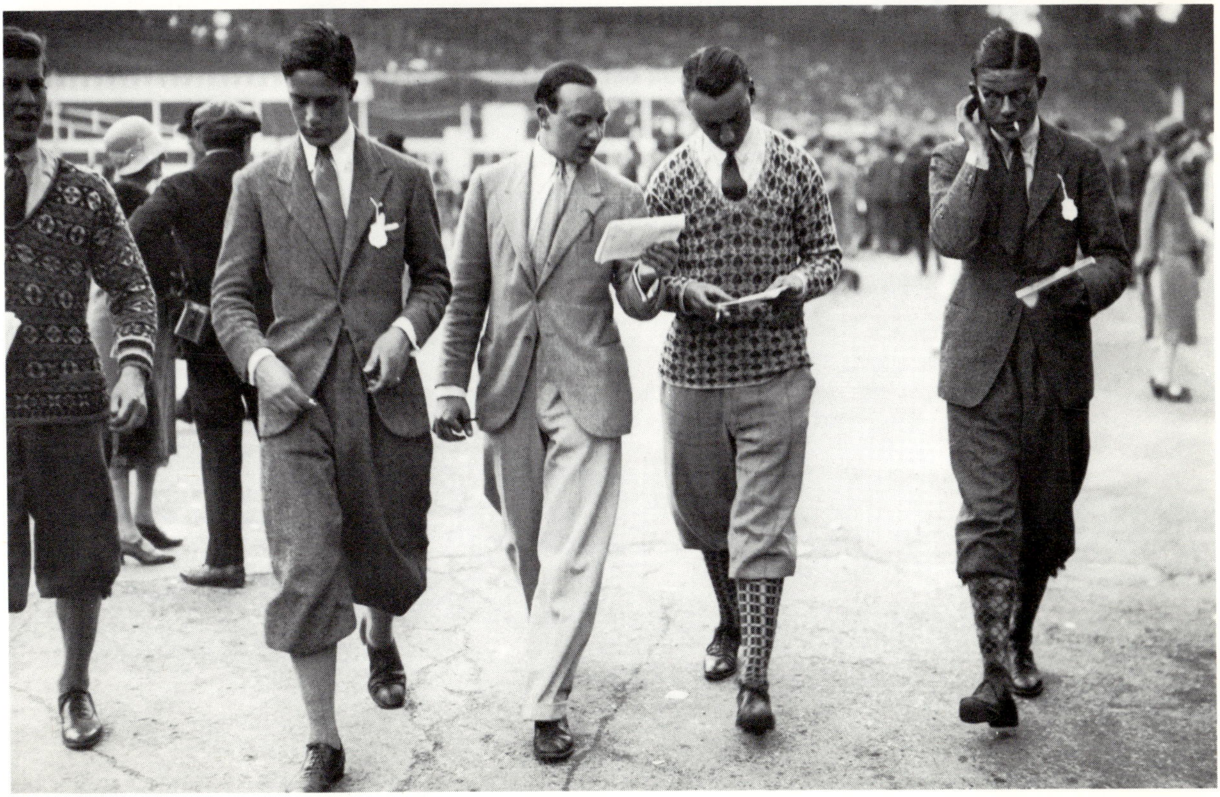

107. Brown and white 'co-respondent' shoes were standard wear for the aspiring 'sheik'; but he might have hesitated to sport the more fanciful models.

108. These tearful girls attended the lying in state of Rudolph Valentino, when he died in New York in 1926.

109. In London members of Valentino's fan club dedicate a shrine to their idol on the roof of the Italian Hospital.

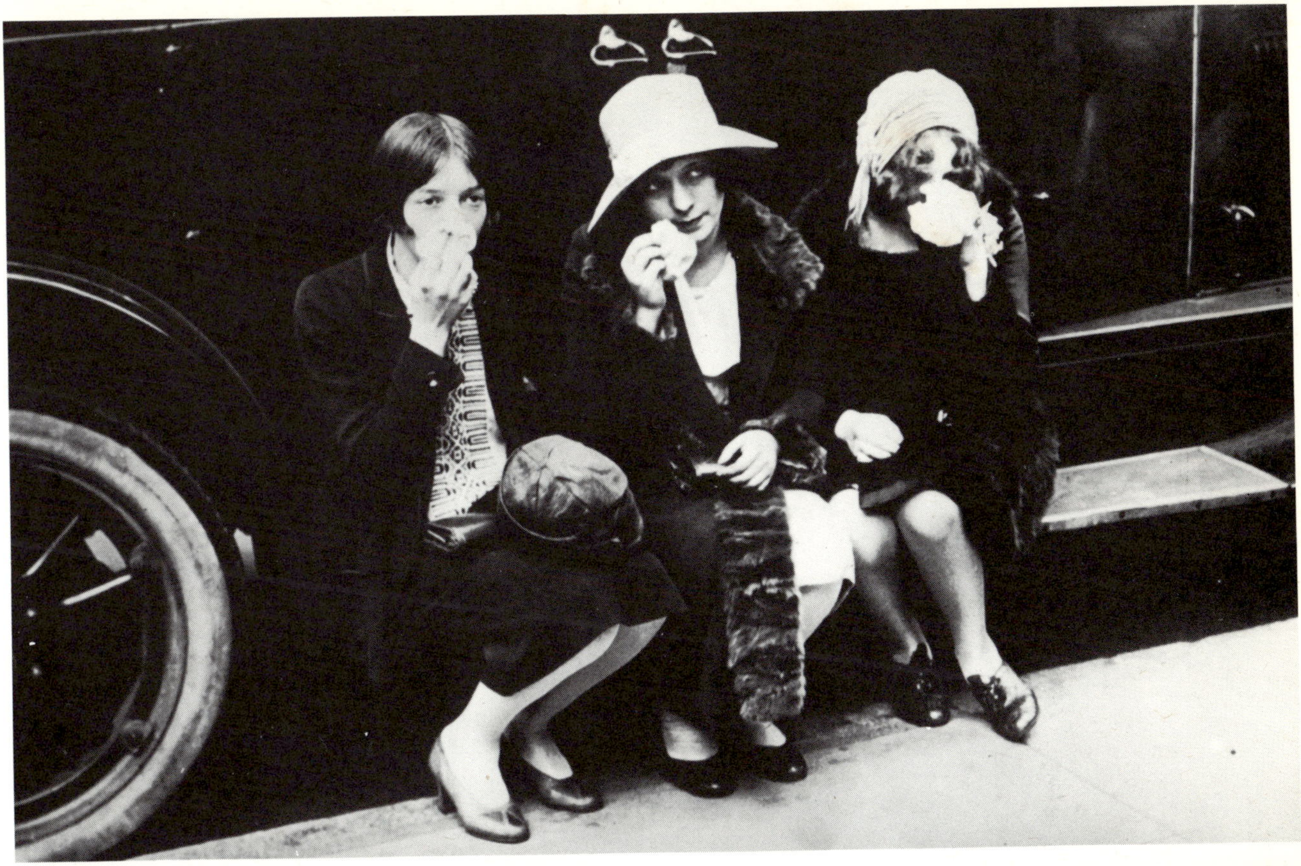

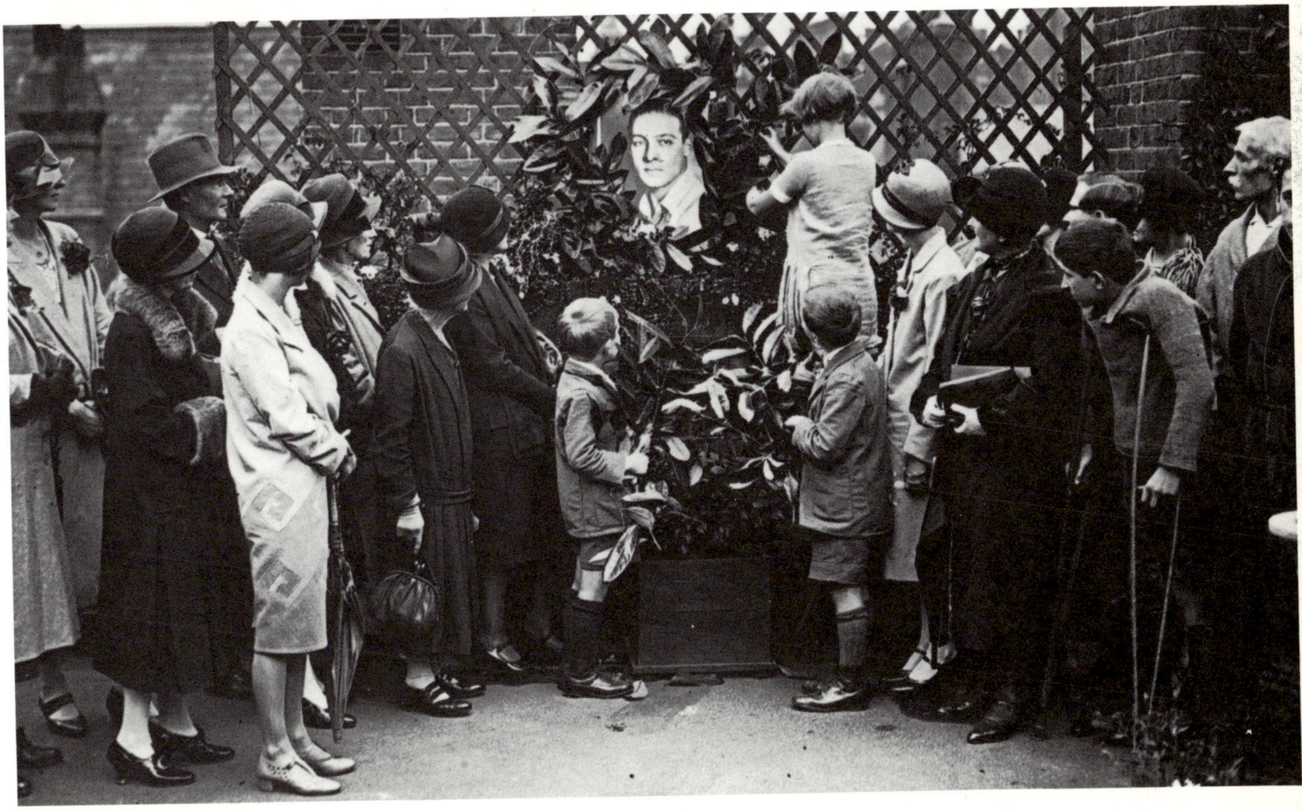

Cocktails for Two in a Room with a View

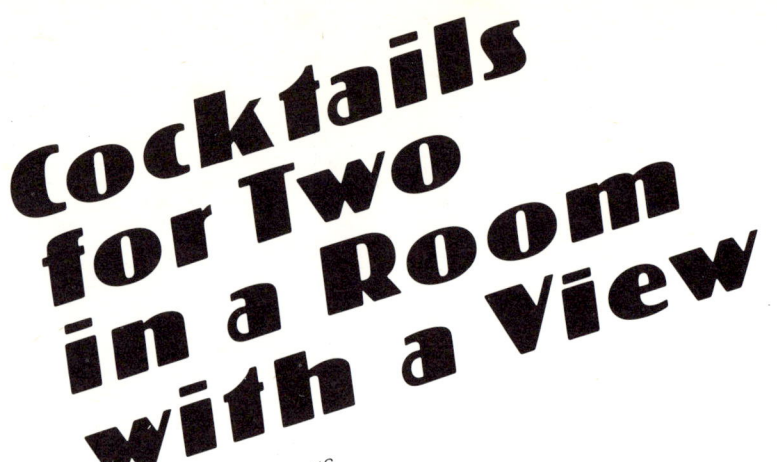

'No-one to worry us,
No-one to hurry us. . . .'

Running in counterpoint to the increasing pace of metropolitan life was a growing desire among large sections of the population to 'Get Away from it All', and, thanks to the proliferation of the cheap motor-car, a good many of them could. More people than ever before went on holidays to the sea-side, and middle-class families could even contemplate the luxury of a Cottage in the Country. In 1924 Francis and Vera Meynell published the Week-end Book, which ran into eighteen impressions by 1930. Half of it was an anthology of poetry for country reading; the other half a compendium of rural pastimes and information, including a list of edible fungi and the songs of wild birds. There was also a collection of country cocktails (Satan's Whisker was one) and a chapter on Party Games, some of them guaranteed to disrupt the cosiest week-end. Along with the quest for fresh air went the new vogue for sun-bathing, and all these pastoral activities could be recorded for ever through the lens of your Brownie.

110. Joan Crawford pleads for yet another cocktail, this time from the wholesome Johnny Mack Brown. The setting — hard angles, shiny surfaces and 'jazz' patterns — is a typical, if exaggerated, 1920s interior.

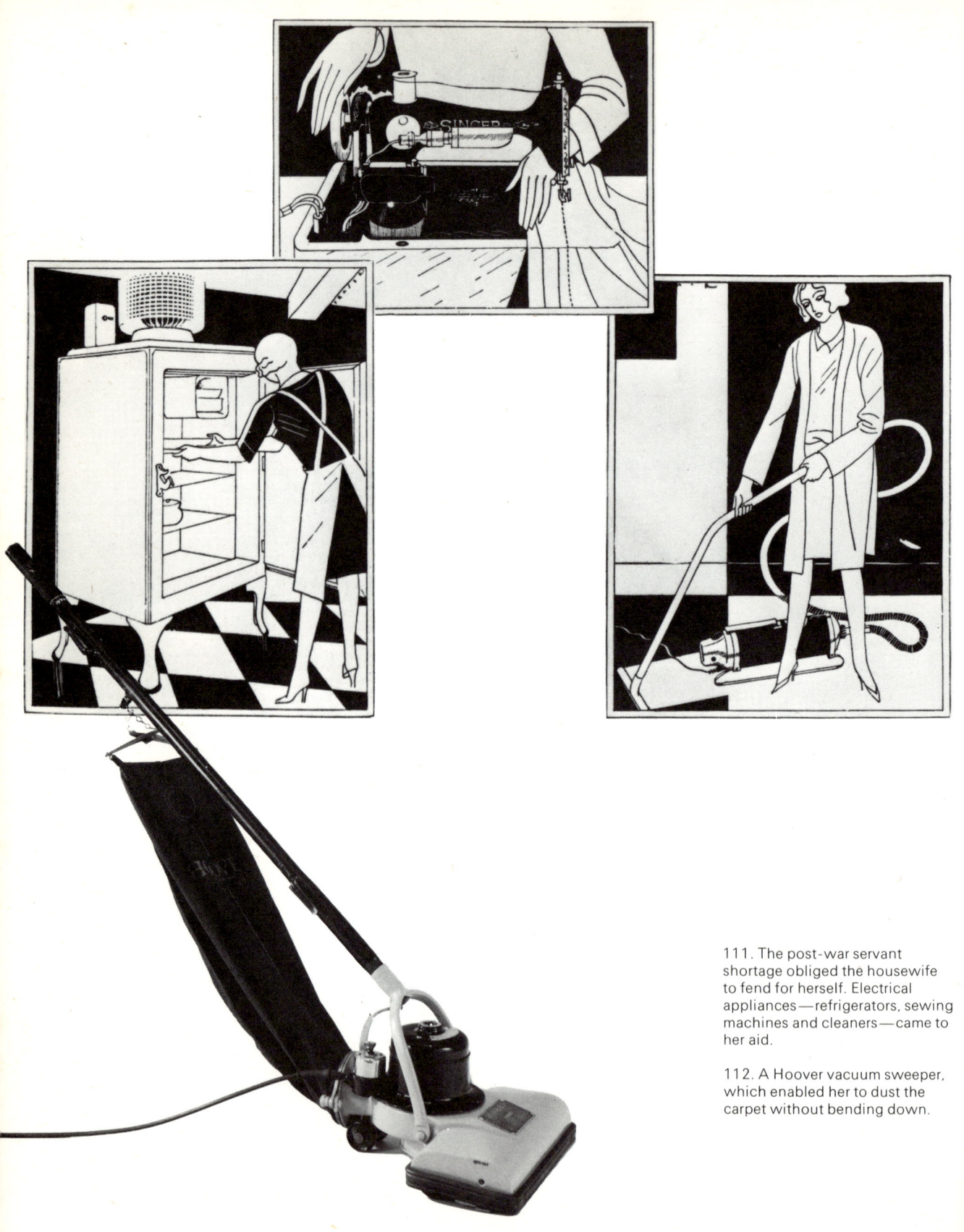

111. The post-war servant shortage obliged the housewife to fend for herself. Electrical appliances—refrigerators, sewing machines and cleaners—came to her aid.

112. A Hoover vacuum sweeper, which enabled her to dust the carpet without bending down.

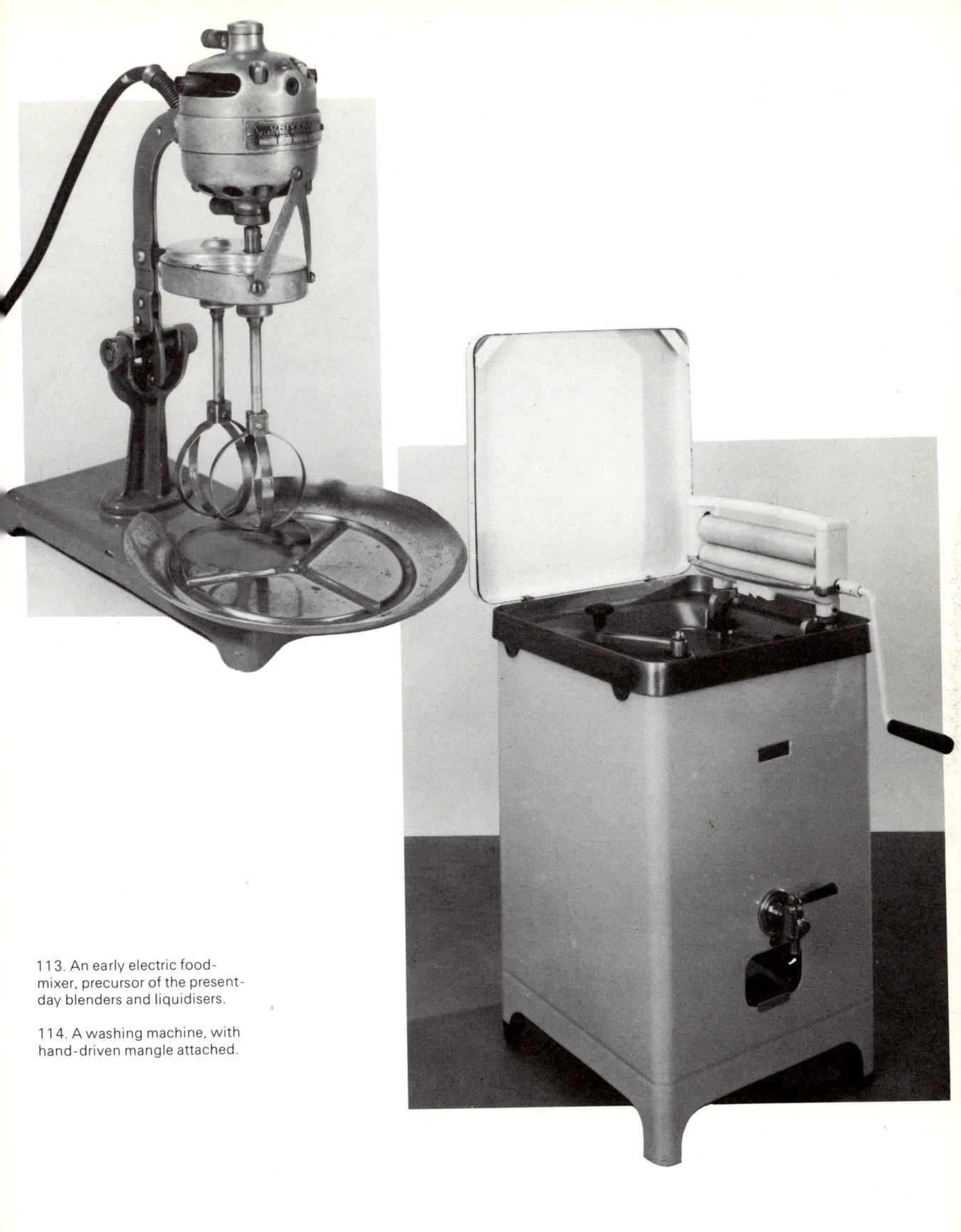

113. An early electric food-mixer, precursor of the present-day blenders and liquidisers.

114. A washing machine, with hand-driven mangle attached.

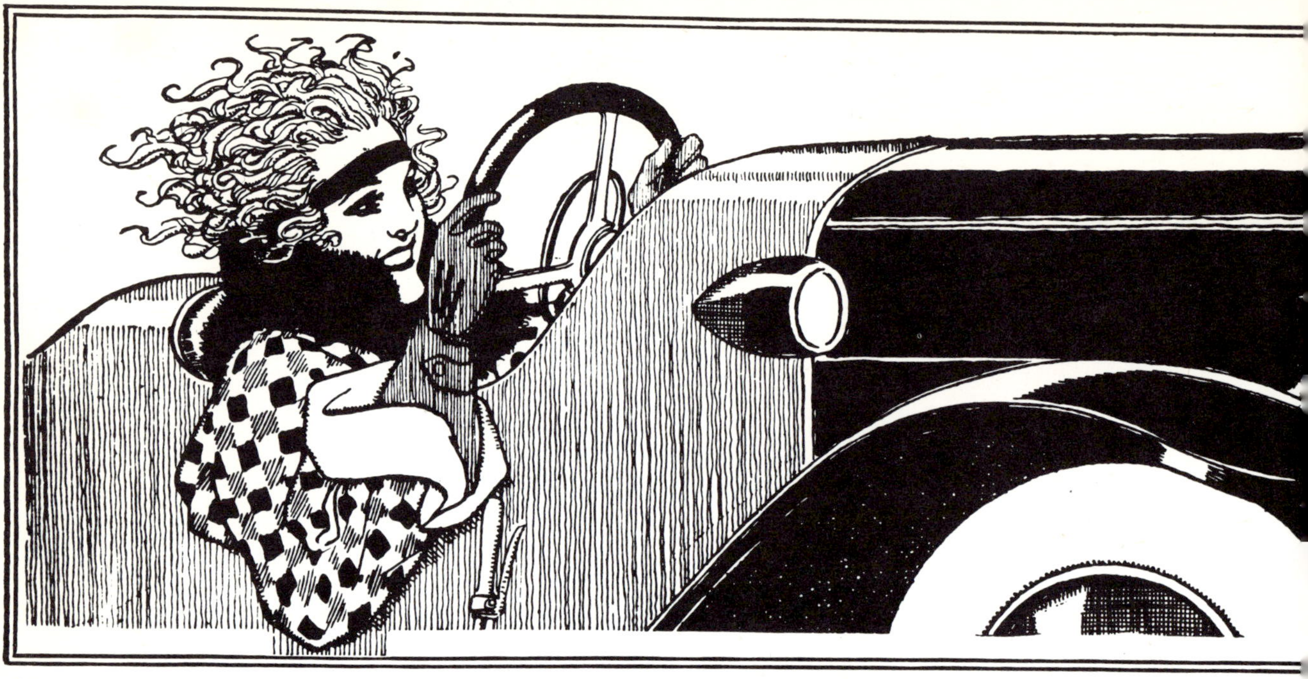

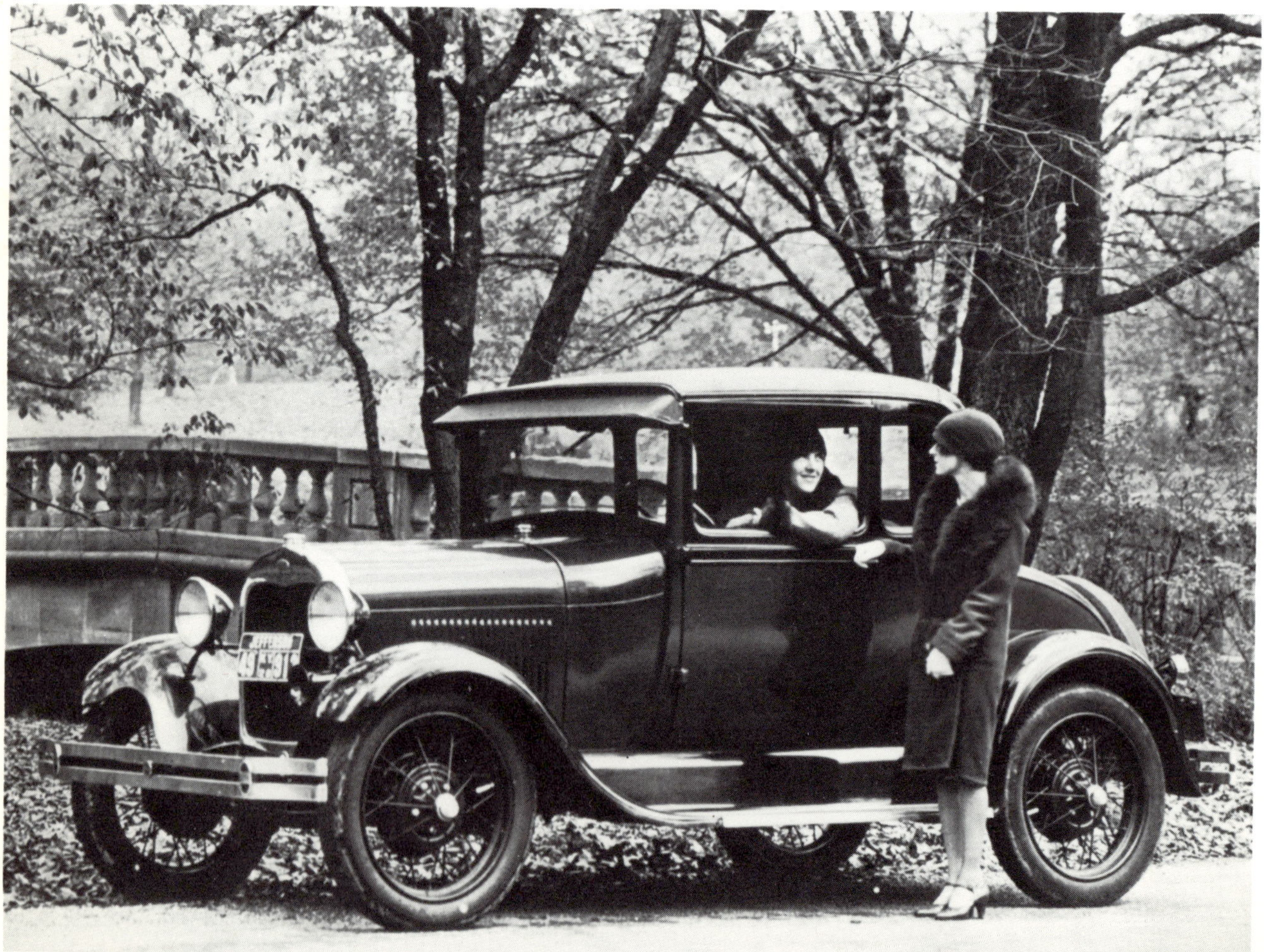

115. The spyker, a sports car thought suitable by the *Tatler* for the lady driver of 1920.

116. This 1927 Model T Ford (bottom left) has a 'dicky' to accommodate two passengers outside.

117. Earlier Model Ts in 1923 and an open 'tourer', with a collapsible hood, for driving in the country.

118. For those who had no car, cheap and increasing public transport provided a means of escape from the cities (right).

119. In London a rapidly expanding underground system led to the installation, at Piccadilly Circus, of automatic ticket machines.

120. Box Hill was a favourite picnic ground for motorists. This democratic party have asked the chauffeur to join them (far right).

121. A picnic on the river, under luxurious conditions, at the Marlow Regatta of 1923.

PICNICS.
TAKE THE MOTOR-BUS FOR PICNICING.

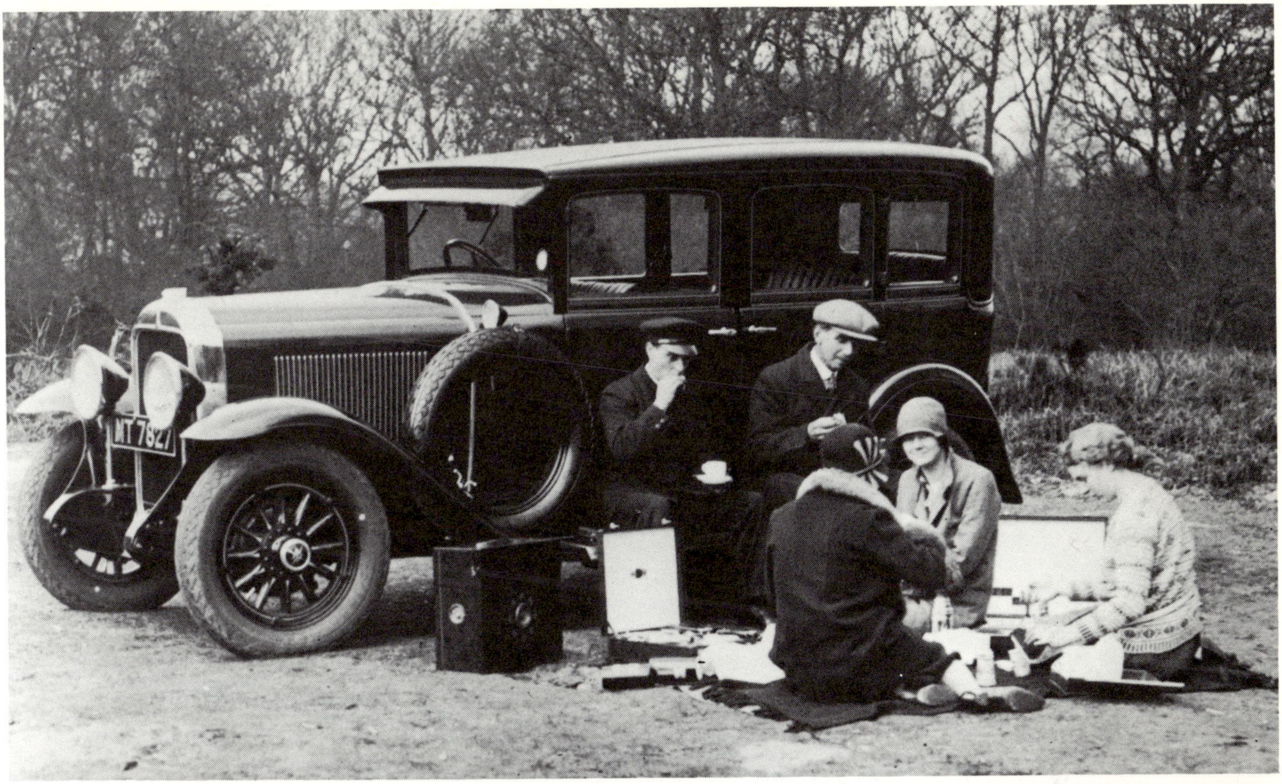
MT 7827

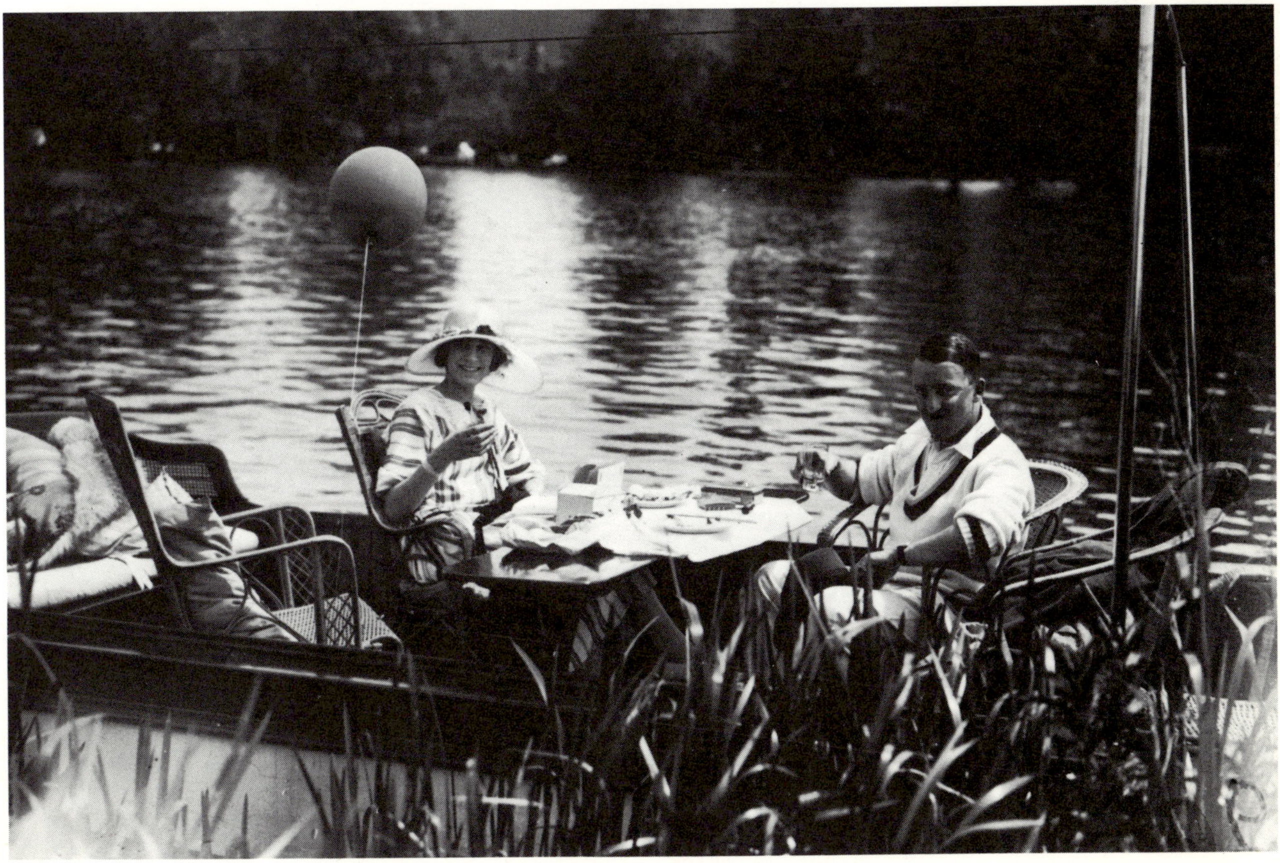

122. By Car to watch Cars: a more informal picnic at Brooklands Race Track.

123. A hot cup of tea after a chilly dip. The rented beach cabin remains a feature of several English sea-side resorts.

124. By the end of the Twenties beachwear had become much briefer, and for the first time since the pre-Victorian era men exposed their torsos—although the girls still wore bathing shoes.

125. The ubiquitous portable gramophone helps to cheer up a rather bleak afternoon on the sand.

126. Cheap cameras enabled everyone to capture holiday scenes for the family snap album.

127. The winner of a photographic competition unpacks his prize, a new camera, before his children's admiring gaze.

128. Fashion photography in 1926. A group of spectators pose at Henley Regatta.

129. His Master's Voice is replaced by His Mistress's Eye.

The Party's Over

'The thrill has gone,
To linger on would spoil it anyhow.
. . .'

Noël Coward, playwright, composer and lyricist, who wrote his first hit, THE VORTEX, at the age of twenty-four, was the authentic voice of the 1920s, and both his style of dialogue— clipped, insouciant and brittle—and the airy brilliance of his music will always evoke the elegant romanticism of the period. In 1928, as if instinctively aware that the Jazz Age was drawing to a close, he took the daring step of composing BITTER SWEET, deliberately harking back to an age which the Twenties had made it their business to despise, and, to many people's astonishment, it was his greatest success. Almost overnight femininity came into fashion again, and at the Paris collections couturiers noticed that women were self-consciously pulling their skirts over their knees as they viewed the new low hemlines. At the end of 1929 came the New York Stock Market Crash, which, starting as a shudder on Wall Street, became an earthquake which shattered the prosperity of the entire Western World. The Party was indeed Over, and the Roaring Twenties ended on a sigh of apprehension and regret.

130. Conservative supporters celebrate the defeat of Labour in 1931 and the formation of a Coalition Government.

131. Party photographs still tended to resemble a School Group: this one includes almost every well-known name on the West End stage.

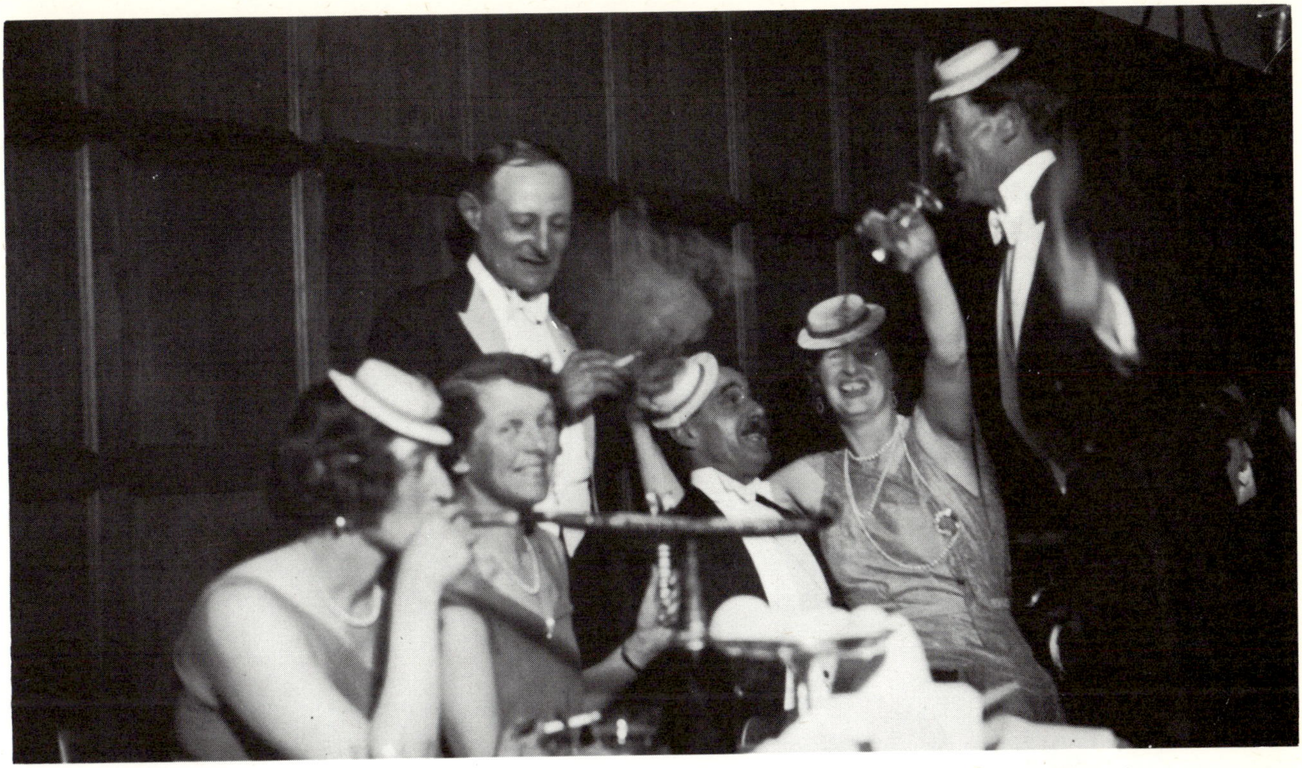

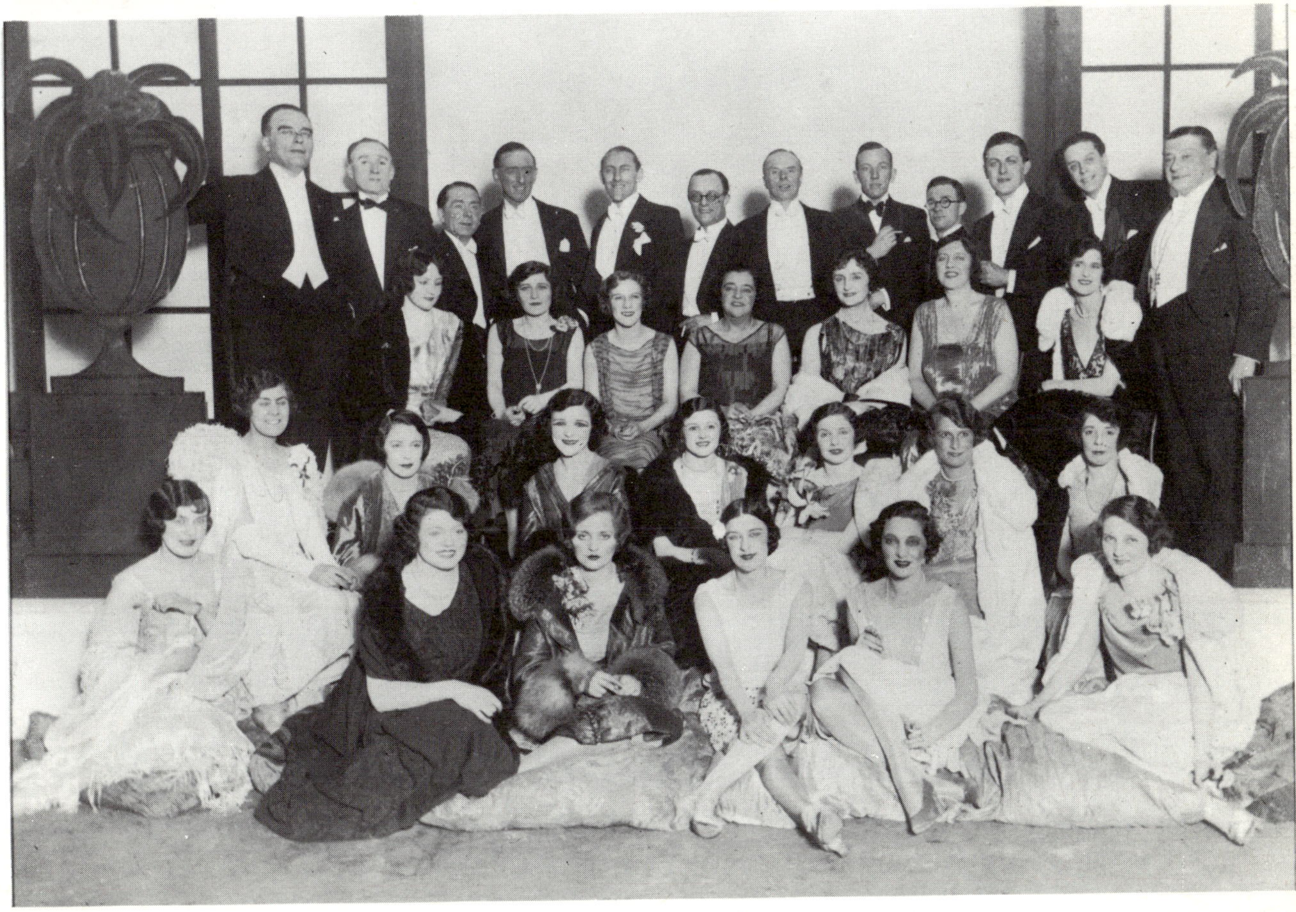

132. 'Baby' parties were a
popular form of entertainment.
The more daring guests filled their
feeding bottles with gin.

133. Fancy dress balls abounded.
This was a Mr J. H. Warrick and
Party, at Kulm Hotel.

134. The Arts Ball at Covent
Garden in 1922. As usual,
Harlequins, Orientals and
Spanish Ladies predominate, but
the blonde in the black hat has
come as, quite simply, Melody.

135. Noël Coward, darling of the Twenties, never hesitated to castigate the age that created him.

136. In 1928 he shrewdly anticipated the return of Romanticism with BITTER SWEET, a sentimental operetta set in the Gay Nineties.

137. The end of the decade saw a revival of Femininity: hair was growing longer and curlier. . . .

138. . . . . and evening dresses echoed the trend with skirts that dipped at the back or fell in flounces to the ankles.

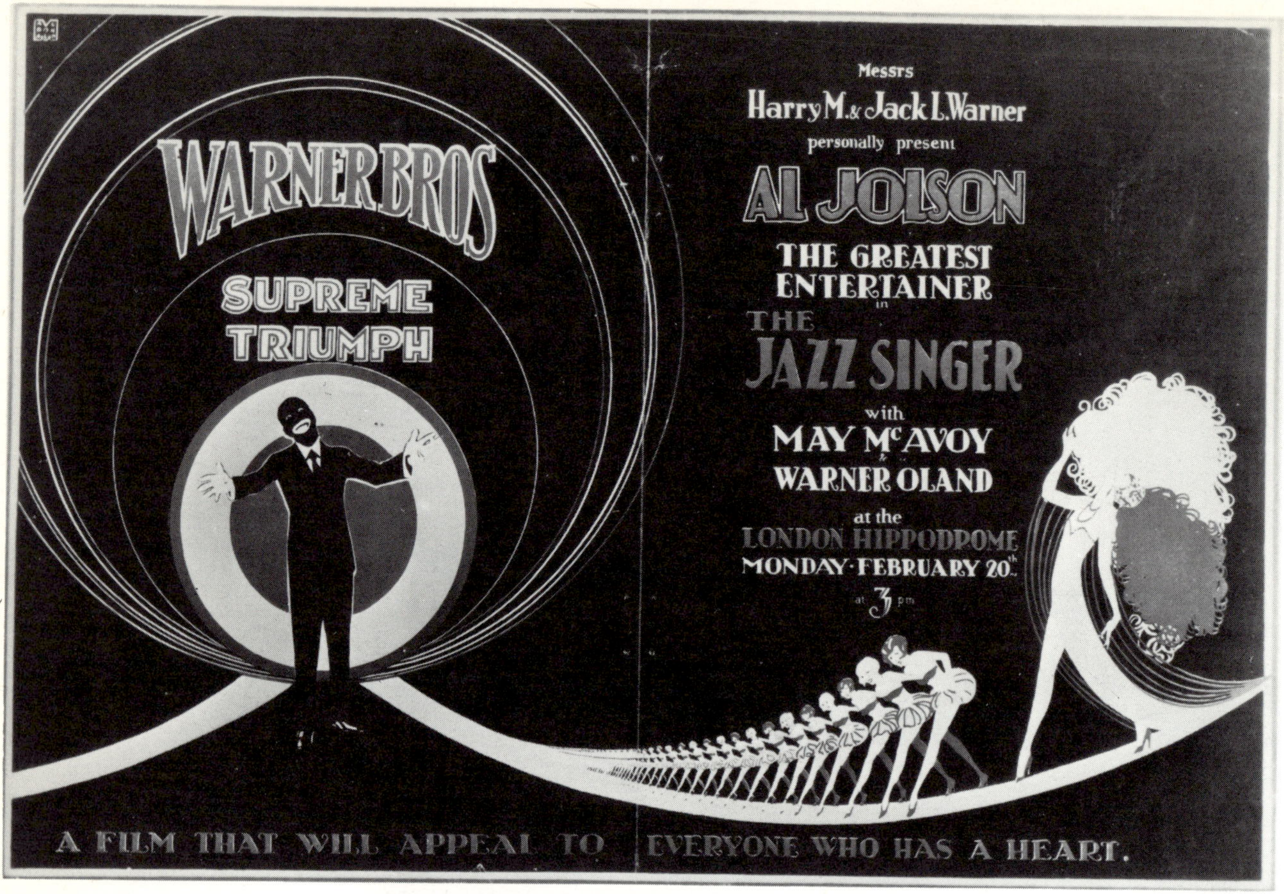

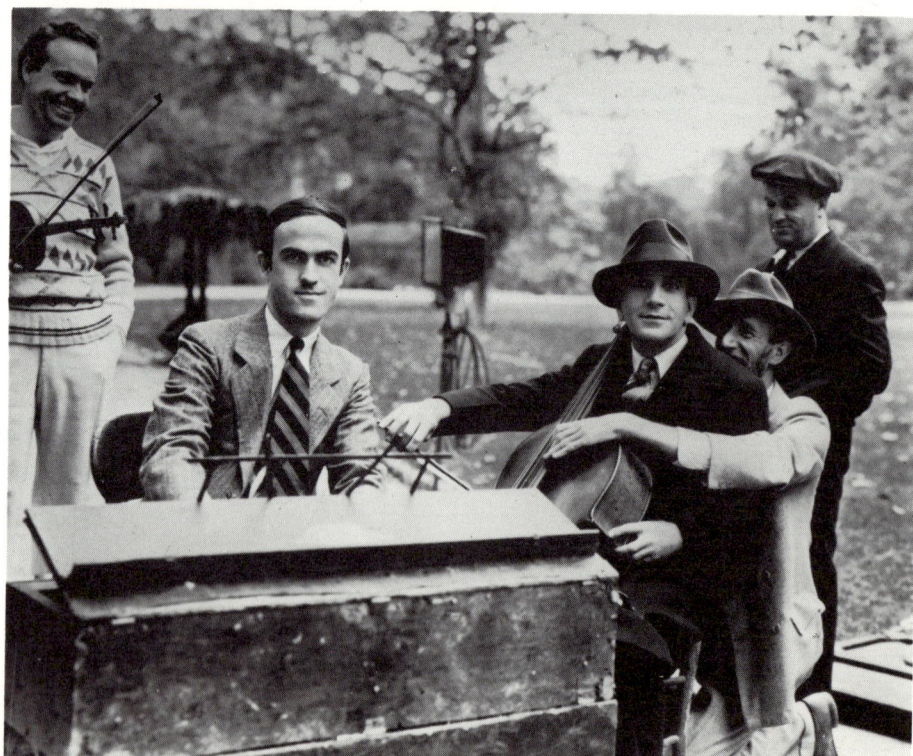

WARNER BROS
SUPREME
TRIUMPH

A FILM THAT WILL APPEAL TO EVERYONE WHO HAS A HEART.

Messrs
Harry M. & Jack L. Warner
personally present
AL JOLSON
THE GREATEST
ENTERTAINER
in
THE
JAZZ SINGER
with
MAY Mc AVOY
&
WARNER OLAND
at the
LONDON HIPPODROME
MONDAY · FEBRUARY 20th
at 3 pm

139. The voice of Al Jolson, saying, 'You ain't heard nothing yet', heralded the end of the Silent Era.

140. Jolson (with cello) clowns with the musicians during the filming of THE JAZZ SINGER.

141. 'All Talking, All Singing, All Dancing' were the new slogans used by film producers to sell their wares.

The Graphic
The National Weekly

THE PRINCE WHO UNDERSTANDS: H.R.H.'s VISIT TO THE DISTRESSED MINING AREAS

THE Prince of Wales tramping the snow-covered lanes of Winlaton, on his tour of the distressed mining areas of Durham, with some of the miners and their wives who acted as his guides. At first hand he thus saw for himself something of the privation, as well as the stoic fortitude, that follows in the wake of long unemployment. The Prince paid house-to-house visits in some of the poorest districts in England, and talked, as man to man, to people who had looked starvation in the

142. The Great War, taboo for most of the decade, suddenly became Box Office with the success of R. C. Sheriff's JOURNEY'S END in 1929.

143. London's Stock Exchange. Although the American Stock Market Crash of 1929 was not repeated here, its effects were increasingly felt as the 1930s progressed.

144. The Prince of Wales embarrassed the Government by saying, during his visit to the distressed mining areas, 'Something must be done' . . . .

145. . . . . But very little was, and by 1931 the number of unemployed had risen to well over two million.